THE LONG SHADOW OF LITTLE ROCK

THE
LONG SHADOW
OF LITTLE ROCK

a memoir by
Daisy Bates

Foreword to the First Edition by Eleanor Roosevelt
Foreword to the Arkansas Edition by Willard B. Gatewood Jr.
Afterword by Clayborne Carson

THE UNIVERSITY OF ARKANSAS PRESS
Fayetteville

Copyright 1986 by Daisy Bates
All rights reserved
Manufactured in the United States of America

ISBN: 978-1-55728-863-9
eISBN: 978-1-61075-247-3

11   10   09   08   07   5   4   3   2

⊛ The paper used in this publication meets the minimum requirements of the
American National Standard for the Permanence of Paper for Printed Library
Materials Z39.48-1984.

The Library of Congress has cataloged the hardcover edition as follows:

Bates, Daisy.
    The long shadow of Little Rock.
    Reprint. Originally published: New York: D. McKay, 1962.
    Includes index.
    1. Bates, Daisy—Childhood and youth. 2. Afro-Americans—Arkansas—
Little Rock—Biography. 3. Little Rock (Ark.)—Biography. 4. School
integration—Arkansas—Little Rock. 5. Little Rock (Ark.) Central High
School. 6. Little Rock (Ark.)—Race relations. I. Title
F419.L7B3 1986 976.7'33 86-19129
ISBN 0-938626-74-4
ISBN 0-938626-75-2 (pbk.)

Dedicated to
The Young Army of
Freedom Fighters

ACKNOWLEDGMENTS

I am grateful to the editors of the *Amsterdam News, New York Post, Arkansas Gazette,* and *Arkansas Democrat* for permission to quote from their publications.

To the author for permission to use his beautiful poem "I Dream a World" from the libretto of *Troubled Island* by Langston Hughes, music by William Grant Still.

For editorial assistance and research to Miss Audre Hanneman, George Bass, Roy Wilkins, Gloster Current, George Penty, Alex Haley, Robert Carter, and Mr. and Mrs. Herbert Birnbaun.

To my husband, L. C., for his enduring faith and encouragement.

There are many others whose counsel and assistance I found invaluable.

CONTENTS

FOREWORD TO THE ARKANSAS EDITION

Daisy Bates's memoir, originally published in 1962, chronicles the moral and physical courage of one who stood at the center of the tumultuous events surrounding the racial integration of Central High School in Little Rock, Arkansas, during 1957–1958. Despite its title, this work is far more than a gripping account of the crisis at Central High. Rather it is the memoir of a remarkable individual whose role in the struggle of Afro-Americans to achieve equal rights culminated, rather than began and ended, in this single episode.

Born and reared in Huttig, a company-owned sawmill town in southern Arkansas, Daisy Lee Gaston never knew her natural parents but she experienced the discrimination and degradation that they and indeed all black people there encountered. Her mother was murdered after refusing the sexual demands of three local white men, and her father left town shortly afterward. Consequently, Daisy grew up in the home of adopted parents with a mother who was religiously devout and a stern taskmaster, and a father who was a strong, proud and loving man. It was her father who bequeathed to her "a lasting inheritance"—the admonition not to hate whites merely because they were white but instead to hate the humiliation, insults and discrimination to which blacks were subjected and to labor to eradicate these injustices. The encounters between Daisy, "the living image" of her biological mother, and her mother's murderer, identified only as "Drunken Pig", are among the most poignant passages in a volume filled with love, hate, fear, pathos and irony. Daisy married L. C. Bates, a friend of her adopted father and a journalist by training, and the couple settled in Little Rock where they became active in the civic life of the black community. By establishing a weekly newspaper, the *Arkansas State Press,* they championed the cause of civil rights of blacks long before the confrontation at Little Rock's high school. Experiences in Huttig, followed by those as a partner in a newspaper and as a leader of the local National Association for the Advancement of Colored People, prepared Daisy Bates for her critical role in the Little Rock crisis. This involvement placed her personal safety in jeopardy and ultimately bankrupted the *Arkansas State Press,* but it helped to bring Afro-Americans a step closer to victory in their long struggle for first class citizenship.

Daisy Bates occupies a place along with Frederick Douglass, W. E. B. Du Bois, Mary Church Terrell, Rosa Parks, Martin Luther King, Jr., and others in the vanguard of movements to transform American ideals into reality. But Mrs. Bates, like other black women who took part in this long struggle, bore a double burden: not only were they considered members of an "inferior" race but also as the "inferior" sex of that race. Despite this double burden, as historian Dorothy Sterling remarked of nineteenth century black women, they "possessed a tenacity of spirit, a gift of endurance, a steadfastness of aspiration that helped a whole population survive." No less than the Sojourner Truths and Harriet Tubmans of the previous century, those of the twentieth century, like Daisy Bates, exhibited a moral courage and single-minded purpose that moved a nation toward recognizing the rights of its largest minority.

For almost a century prior to the launching of the *Arkansas State Press* by Daisy and L. C. Bates, black women had been involved in journalism as editors, publishers and contributors. As early as the 1850s Mary Ann Shadd Cary, reputedly the first black "editress" in North America, established and managed the *Provincial Freeman.* In the tradition of Cary, black women journalists following her utilized their columns in behalf of Afro-Americans and their rights. Of her predecessors in the cause of black civil rights, Daisy Bates's career perhaps most closely parallels that of Ida B. Wells Barnett who, born in Mississippi in 1862, was a journalist and co-owner of the *Free Press* in Memphis. So outspoken did the weekly become in its criticism of Southern lynching that her office was destroyed, and she was driven from the city. Undaunted, she took to the lecture circuit and denounced lynching in hundreds of speeches throughout the United States and Great Britain. In 1895 she, like Daisy Bates, married a man several years her senior, Ferdinand L. Barnett, the publisher of a black newspaper in Chicago. As did Ferdinand Barnett, L. C. Bates also enthusiastically supported the civil rights activities of his wife. In little more than a decade after Ida Well Barnett's death in 1929, Daisy Bates, the product of a small town on the other side of the Mississippi, assumed her mantle by becoming an effective and articulate advocate of racial justice. During the Little Rock crisis, she demonstrated how thoroughly she had embraced the tradition bequeathed by Mary Shadd Cary, Ida Wells Barnett and other black women of the nineteenth century.

Since the original publication of this memoir, Daisy Bates has been honored throughout the United States for her role in the struggle that challenged Americans to confront the disparity between the profession and practice of their ideals of liberty, justice, democracy and equality. Notwithstanding such honors and recognition, she refused to abandon her struggle, because she fully understood that the crisis at Central High School represented only a successful skirmish, not a victorious conclusion to a long war. Through her activities since 1962, including the revival of the *Arkansas State Press,* she continues to devote her energies to the cause of winning for Afro-Americans the justice, dignity and respect that rightfully belong to all citizens. Thirty years after the confrontation at Little Rock, the name of Daisy Bates still invites images of a crusader in the best American tradition, of one armed with the Declaration of Independence, the Constitution and compassion for humanity whose goals are justice and freedom for all Americans regardless of race or color.

WILLARD B. GATEWOOD, JR.
June 1986

FOREWORD TO THE FIRST EDITION

This is a book which I hope will be read by every American. It is simply told and easy to read, but not pleasant. Gathered together here is a chronicle day by day of what happened in what would ordinarily be considered a rather progressive, pleasant, medium-sized city in the U.S. It happened because of the actions of a highly prejudiced, unthinking governor. He called out all the worst side of other prejudiced individuals throughout his area of the States.

Within all of us there are two sides. One reaches for the stars, the other descends to the level of the beasts. The picture of the mobs in Little Rock, and later in other areas of the South, shows clearly that the beast in us was predominant. The record of burning crosses, bombings, shootings, etc., is a record of the beast on the march. No one in authority in this city of Little Rock tried to control and draw out the best in people instead of the worst. This is the sad thing about it. Not even the few coura-geous ministers could kindle even a spark of courage which would have turned the tide. We do not yet seem to have learned the lesson that where there is prejudice and oppression in one area it invariably spreads in many other areas. It may not happen today or tomorrow but surely at some point it will erupt and there will be a new reason for the beast to march. This is seen in history.

As you read this story where all the incidents are drawn together, you marvel at the courage of the Colored community, but you marvel even more at the courage of the few white people who fought down the beast and remained human beings. There were even a few white children who had this courage. Of course it seems to me nothing short of a miracle that the nine Negro children had the stamina to live through this period and their parents must have suffered even more than they did. To give your child for a cause is even harder than to give yourself.

The hardest part of the story is the change brought about in young people by the influence of their elders. The story shows how at the beginning a Colored girl who was attractive and could sing, was asked to join the Glee Club, and some of the other children were asked to join some of the white children at lunch. Gradually, however, the atmosphere changed. The parents had been at work. The children could have found a way to live together but the parents would not let them. Then the beast took over in the children, and children can be cruel. They can devise all kinds of tortures and enjoy them, and here the beast within them was being praised and they were looked upon as heroes at home.

I wish that Mrs. Bates who suffered so much and had such courage throughout all her difficulties, who could bear to see with her husband their life's work destroyed and still go on and work for the cause she believed in, had been able to keep from giving us some of the sense of her bitterness and fear in the end of her book. Given the circumstances, this was almost too much to expect even from such a fine person. I have paid her homage in my thoughts many times and I want to tell her again how remarkable I think she was through these horrible years. I only hope that before too long the people of my race in my country will wake up to the fact that they are endangering the peace of the world. The world is made up of people of many races and many colors. They must be accepted as people and treated with the same dignity and respect wherever they are. Until we do this with our own citizens at home we will be suspect to the world, our leadership will have little value and we will endanger the peace of the world because we have the responsibility to give an example of how nations can live together in peace and unity.

This book should shock the conscience of America and bring a realization of where we stand in the year 1962 in these United States.

Eleanor Roosevelt

ELEANOR ROOSEVELT

THE LONG SHADOW OF LITTLE ROCK

CHAPTER I

LITTLE ROCK

Until a September day in 1957 Little Rock was a quiet, undistinguished southern city, notable principally as being the capital of the State of Arkansas and for having won several national awards for being one of the cleanest cities of its size. Then suddenly it became a term heard around the world, a milestone like Lexington and Concord in man's long struggle for freedom and justice.

Even after the words "Little Rock" were on everyone's lips, few bothered to locate the city on the map. Those who went to the trouble would have found it located close to the geographical center of Arkansas. It is bounded on the north by the Arkansas River and on the south by low, granite-based hills. To the east lies open farming country, and to the west beautiful homes nestle in the shadows of gently rolling hills. The city itself rests on fairly level ground.

The city's hundred thousand citizens, Negroes and whites, took pride in the physical beauty of their town and for many years had lived side by side with little surface friction. The city had a progressive Public Housing Authority that made it possible for low income families—Negro and white—to move into well-appointed, but segregated, public housing. There was also a good, but segregated, school system with several modern educational plants of recent construction.

The tragedy that placed Little Rock on the world stage centered around Central High School located in the heart of the city. The school was built in 1927 at a cost of $1,500,000. It is an impressive structure, rising from landscaped grounds like a small university in yellow-bricked grandeur. It accommodates possibly three thousand pupils in a hundred classrooms built on seven levels. For years it has enjoyed the highest academic rating given by the North Central Association of Colleges and Secondary Schools. Two of its graduates have become Rhodes scholars.

For many years prior to the unfolding of the events I am about to describe, race relations in the city had been relatively calm and improving. By this I do not mean there had not been many incidents of police brutality toward Negroes, and that the vicious southern system of relegating the black population to the role of secondary citizens had not been maintained in full force. But a spirit of calm pervaded the atmosphere, and there was a notable lack of tension.

My husband, L. C. Bates, and I had moved to Little Rock

in 1941 and started a newspaper, the *State Press*. In spite of its crusading spirit, the paper prospered; and L. C., as my husband was always known, looked forward to a life of, if not serenity, at least quiet, progressive, journalistic endeavor. We had, of course, hailed the 1954 Supreme Court decision on school integration as a great forward step in achieving true equality for our race; and we felt the school board of Little Rock, while moving all too slowly, was determined to obey the law at least in token form and make a start on integration according to plans it had formulated and announced well in advance.

The plans called for the entrance into Central High School of nine Negro pupils when school opened on September 4, 1957. The city had apparently accepted the board's plans; and there seemed little reason to expect serious opposition, much less what followed. The summer passed quickly for those of us active in the National Association for the Advancement of Colored People in preparing the children selected for this initial move toward integration to hold their own academically. And almost before I knew it, we were deep into August and the opening of school but a few weeks away.

On the evening of August 22, I was sitting in my living room listening to the eleven o'clock news broadcast on television. I heard the announcer say:

"Governor Marvin Griffin, of Georgia, and Roy V. Harris, two of the South's most ardent segregationists, tonight addressed a state-wide meeting." The report continued that approximately three hundred fifty persons attended the dinner and heard Governor Griffin attack the Supreme Court decision and praise the courage of the Arkansas groups who were fighting to preserve the rights of states. He referred to them as "patriots." He urged the support of a national propaganda campaign to support their stand. The announcer went on to state that the Capital Citizens Council, a local segregationist group, was host, and that while the Governor of Arkansas, Orval Eugene Faubus, had not attended the meeting, he would entertain Governor Griffin at breakfast the following morning.

After the broadcast I took Skippy, our dog, for his nightly walk. Little did I realize that this would be the last quiet walk that Skippy and I would enjoy for many years.

After we re-entered the house, I sat down on the divan in the living room, directly in front of our large picture window, and started glancing through the newspaper. Suddenly a large object came crashing through the glass. Instinctively I threw myself on the floor. I was covered with shattered glass. L. C. rushed into the room. He bent over me as I lay on the floor. "Are you hurt? Are you hurt?" he cried.

"I don't think so," I said uncertainly. I reached for the rock lying in the middle of the floor. A note was tied to it. I broke the string and unfolded a soiled piece of paper. Scrawled in bold print were the words: STONE THIS TIME. DYNAMITE NEXT.

I handed the note to L. C. "A message from the Arkansas *patriots*," I remarked. As he left the room to telephone the police, I heard L. C. say, "Thank God their aim was poor."

Suddenly I realized that this calm I had so taken for granted was only the calm before the storm, that this was war, and that as State President of the National Association for the Advancement of Colored People I was in the front-line trenches. Was I ready for war? Was I ready to risk everything that L. C. and I had built? Who was I really and what did I

4

stand for? Long after I had gone to bed my mind ranged over these questions and over the whole course of my life. Toward dawn I knew I had found the answer. I was ready. I drifted off into the sleep of a mind no longer torn by doubt or indecision.

CHAPTER II

REBIRTH

I was born Daisy Lee Gatson in the little sawmill town of Huttig, in southern Arkansas. The owners of the mill ruled the town. Huttig might have been called a sawmill plantation, for everyone worked for the mill, lived in houses owned by the mill, and traded at the general store run by the mill.

The hard, red clay streets of the town were mostly unnamed. Main Street, the widest and longest street in town, and the muddiest after a rain, was the site of our business square. It consisted of four one-story buildings which housed a commissary and meat market, a post office, an ice cream parlor, and a movie house. Main Street also divided "White Town" from "Negra Town." However, the physical appearance of the two areas provided a more definite means of distinction.

The Negro citizens of Huttig were housed in rarely painted, drab red "shotgun" houses, so named because one could stand in the front yard and look straight through the front and back doors into the back yard. The Negro community was also provided with two church buildings of the same drab red exterior, although kept spotless inside by the Sisters of the church, and a two-room schoolhouse equipped with a potbellied stove that never quite succeeded in keeping it warm.

On the other side of Main Street were white bungalows, white steepled churches and a white spacious school with a big lawn. Although the relations between Negro and white were cordial, the tone of the community, as indicated by outward appearances, was of the "Old South" tradition.

As I grew up in this town, I knew I was a Negro, but I did not really understand what that meant until I was seven years old. My parents, as do most Negro parents, protected me as long as possible from the inevitable insult and humiliation that is, in the South, a part of being "colored."

I was a proud and happy child—all hair and legs, my cousin Early B. used to say—and an only child, although not blessed with the privilege of having my way. One afternoon, shortly after my seventh birthday, my mother called me in from play.

"I'm not feeling well," she said. "You'll have to go to the market to get the meat for dinner."

I was thrilled with such an important errand. I put on one of my prettiest dresses and my mother brushed my hair. She gave me a dollar and instructions to get a pound of center-cut pork chops. I skipped happily all the way to the market.

When I entered the market, there were several white adults waiting to be served. When the butcher had finished with them, I gave him my order. More white adults entered. The butcher turned from me and took their orders. I was a little annoyed but felt since they were grownups it was all right. While he was waiting on the adults, a little white girl came in and we talked while we waited.

The butcher finished with the adults, looked down at us and asked, "What do you want, little girl?" I smiled and said, "I told you before, a pound of center-cut pork chops." He snarled, "I'm not talking to you," and again asked the white girl what she wanted. She also wanted a pound of center-cut pork chops.

"Please may I have my meat?" I said, as the little girl left. The butcher took my dollar from the counter, reached into the showcase, got a handful of fat chops and wrapped them up. Thrusting the package at me, he said, "Niggers have to wait 'til I wait on the white people. Now take your meat and get out of here!" I ran all the way home crying.

When I reached the house, my mother asked what had happened. I started pulling her toward the door, telling her what the butcher had said. I opened the meat and showed it to her. "It's fat, Mother. Let's take it back."

"Oh, Lord, I knew I shouldn't have sent her. Stop crying now, the meat isn't so bad."

"But it is. Why can't we take it back?"

"Go on out on the porch and wait for Daddy." As she turned from me, her eyes were filling with tears.

When I saw Daddy approaching, I ran to him, crying. He lifted me in his arms and smiled. "Now, what's wrong?" When I told him, his smile faded.

8

"And if we don't hurry, the market will be closed," I finished.

"We'll talk about it after dinner, sweetheart." I could feel his muscles tighten as he carried me into the house.

Dinner was distressingly silent. Afterward my parents went into the bedroom and talked. My mother came out and told me my father wanted to see me. I ran into the bedroom. Daddy sat there, looking at me for a long time. Several times he tried to speak, but the words just wouldn't come. I stood there, looking at him and wondering why he was acting so strangely. Finally he stood up and the words began tumbling from him. Much of what he said I did not understand. To my seven-year-old mind he explained as best he could that a Negro had no rights that a white man respected.

He dropped to his knees in front of me, placed his hands on my shoulders, and began shaking me and shouting.

"Can't you understand what I've been saying?" he demanded. "There's nothing I can do! If I went down to the market I would only cause trouble for my family."

As I looked at my daddy sitting by me with tears in his eyes, I blurted out innocently, "Daddy, are you afraid?"

He sprang to his feet in an anger I had never seen before. "Hell, no! I'm not afraid for myself, I'm not afraid to die. I could go down to that market and tear him limb from limb with my bare hands, but I am afraid for you and your mother."

That night when I knelt to pray, instead of my usual prayers, I found myself praying that the butcher would die. After that night we never mentioned him again.

Shortly after my eighth birthday I was playing with other children on a neighbor's steps. An older boy, whom I didn't happen to like, came up and began pulling my braids. I said

I was going home. The boy said, "You always act so uppity. If you knew what happened to your mother, you wouldn't act so stuck up."

"Nothing's wrong with my mother," I retorted. "I just left her."

"I'm talking about your *real* mother, the one the white man took out and killed."

"That's a story and you're a mean and nasty old boy!" I began to cry.

"It ain't. I heard my folks talking about it."

Just then the mother of one of my playmates came out on the porch and yelled at the boy. "Shut up! You talk too much. I'm going to tell your mother, and you'll get the beating of your life.

"Honey," she said to me, "don't believe nothing that no-good boy says." Still, I wondered what if he was telling me the truth?

At dinner that evening I looked intently at my parents, all the while trying to decide whether I looked like them. I could see no resemblance or likeness to myself in either of them. I remembered many little things, like the day Mother was talking to a salesman when I came in. He glanced at me, then turned to my mother.

"Have you heard from her father?" he had asked her.

When my mother said she hadn't, the salesman nodded toward me. "Does she know?"

"We haven't told her," my mother had said.

During the next few weeks I kept so much to myself that my parents decided that I must be sick. So I was "dosed" up with little pink pills. My cousin Early B. came to visit us. He was several years older than I, but I was always glad to see him because he protected me from the boys who liked to taunt and tease me.

One afternoon as we walked along the millpond, I asked Early B. to tell me about my mother. He looked at me puzzled.

"Your mother?" he said guardedly, and pointed in the direction of my house. We could see her sitting on the porch.

"No. I mean my *real* mother."

"You know?"

"Yes."

"Everything?"

"Well, almost."

"Who told you? I'll knock his block off! Have you told your mamma and papa?"

"No."

We walked on in silence until we stood on the bank that divided the millpond from the town's fishing hole. Large logs floated in the water. The smell of fresh-cut lumber mixed with the odor of dead fish. As we stood there, Early B. told me of my parents.

"One night when you were a baby and your daddy was working nights at the mill, a man went to your house and told your mother that your daddy had been hurt. She rushed out, leaving you alone, but she met a neighbor and asked her to listen out for you while she went to see about your daddy.

"When your daddy got home the next morning, he found you alone. He went around asking the neighbors if they had seen your mother. The neighbor your mother had asked to look after you told him what happened the night before—that she saw a man who looked like he was colored, although she didn't get a good look at him because he was walking in front of your mother.

"The news spread fast around town that your mother couldn't be found. Later in the morning, some people out fishing found her body."

Early B. stopped talking and sat down on the pond bank. I stood over him, looking into the dark, muddy water.

"Where did they find her?" I asked.

After a long silence Early B. pointed at the water and said, "Right down there. She was half in and half out."

"Who did it?"

"Well," he answered, "there was a lot of talk from the cooks and cleaning women who worked in 'white town' about what they had heard over there. They said that three white men did it."

"What happened to my father?"

"He was so hurt, he left you with the people who have you now, his best friends. He left town. Nobody has heard from him since."

"What did my real parents look like?"

"They were young. Your daddy was as light as a lot of white people. Your mother was very pretty—dark brown, with long black hair."

Early B.'s friends came along and he wandered off with them. I sat there looking into the dark waters, vowing that some day I would get the men who killed my mother. I did not realize that the afternoon had turned into evening and darkness had closed in around me until someone sitting beside me whispered, "It's time to go home, darling." I turned and saw my daddy sitting beside me. He reached out in the darkness and took my hand.

"How long have you known?" he asked.

"A long time," I said.

He lifted me tenderly in his arms and carried me home.

12

The next morning I had a high temperature. I remember the neighbors coming in, talking in quiet tones. That afternoon a playmate brought me a little box holding three guinea pigs. At first I thought they were rats. Knowing my mother's fear of rats, I hid the box in my bed.

That night the Church Sisters, who met each week at the church or at the home of some sick person to pray, gathered at our home. They knelt around my bed and prayed for my soul. I noticed the fat knees of one praying lady. It gave me an idea I couldn't resist. I eased the box to the floor and released the guinea pigs. One of them ran across the fat lady's leg. Unable to lift her weight up on the chair beside her, she lumbered around the room, screaming hysterically. The other ladies, managing to keep a few paces ahead of her, joined in the wild demonstration.

Above the hubbub I heard my mother's voice sternly demanding to know where the creatures came from. Helpless with laughter, I could not reply. The guinea pigs broke up the prayer meeting and I got my behind properly spanked. The ladies, although convinced that I certainly needed prayer, decided to do their praying for me elsewhere.

In Arkansas, even in the red clay soil of a mill town, flowers grow without any encouragement at all. Everyone's yard had some sort of flowering bush or plant all spring and summer. And in this town of Huttig, where there was so little beauty, I passionately loved all blooming things. In the woods I hunted out the first of the cowslips and spring beauties, and from open fields, the last of the Indian paintbrush. I was always bringing home bouquets.

All of the neighbors knew that the flowers in our yard were

my garden, not Mother's. I had no favorites and delighted at each flower in its season. When the last roses and zinnias had died, I knew in a few short months the old lilac bush would start budding, for winter in Arkansas is short-lived. But this year was different. One morning I was out before breakfast looking for flowers to pick. All I found was a single red rose, the dew still wet on it. I can close my eyes today and see exactly how it looked. Unaccountably I turned, leaving it on its stalk, and walked into the house crying.

My mother met me at the door and I saw her face cloud with anxiety. What was the trouble? "All the other flowers were dead," I sobbed, "and my rose will die, too."

That night I heard her say to Daddy, "I can't understand that child, crying over a dying flower." Then I heard my daddy say, "Let her be. It just takes time."

My family had not spoken to me of my real mother since that day the ladies came to pray for me.

Later in the fall, on a Saturday afternoon, my father and I took a walk in the woods. It was a brisk day. Daddy thought we might find some ripe persimmons. Also, some black walnuts might have fallen from a big old tree he knew about. We walked along sniffing the air, sharp with the smell of pine needles, then came out in an open stretch in sight of the persimmon grove. I was always happy on these excursions with Daddy. I guess it was just the feeling that I couldn't be happy now, couldn't let myself be, that made me ask the question.

"Daddy, who killed my mother? Why did they kill her?"

We walked on a little way in silence. Then he pointed to some flat rocks on a slope, and we made our way there and rested. The persimmons and walnuts were forgotten. He began in tones so soft I could barely hear the words.

14

He told me of the timeworn lust of the white man for the Negro woman—which strikes at the heart of every Negro man in the South. I don't remember a time when this man I called my father didn't talk to me almost as if I were an adult. Even so, this was a difficult concept to explain to an eight-year-old girl; but he spoke plainly, in simple words I could understand. He wanted me to realize that my mother wouldn't have died if it hadn't been for her race—as well as her beauty, her pride, her love for my father.

"Your mother was not the kind to submit," he said, "so they took her." His voice grew bitter. "They say that three white men did it. There was some talk about who they were, but no one knew for sure, and the sheriff's office did little to find out."

He said some other things about the way the Negro is treated in the South, but my mind had stopped, fastening on those three white men and what they had done. They had killed my mother.

When we walked out of the woods, my daddy looked tired and broken. He took my hand and we walked home in silence.

Dolls, games, even my once-beloved fishing, held little interest for me after that. Young as I was, strange as it may seem, my life now had a secret goal—to find the men who had done this horrible thing to my mother. So happy once, now I was like a little sapling which, after a violent storm, puts out only gnarled and twisted branches.

School opened. Nothing had changed. We had the same worn-out textbooks handed down to us from the white school. With the first frosts the teacher wrestled with the potbellied stove. Days drifted by as we tried to gain an education in these

15

surroundings. One afternoon my mother sent me to the commissary, where one could purchase anything from a nail to an automobile. Just as I reached the store, I saw some of my friends approaching. I paused on the step to wait for them. As I stood there waiting, I felt someone staring at me. I turned around and looked into the face of a rather young white man sitting on one of the benches on the porch that ran the entire length of the store. We stared at each other for a long time. I have read descriptions of the contest in staring which a bird and a snake will carry on. The two of us must have presented such a picture, although considering my own feelings I don't know which of us symbolized the snake and which the bird.

Finally my friends called to me. I turned and entered the store with them. Once inside I looked back. The white man's eyes were still fixed on me.

People who knew my mother said I was "the living image of her." As I stood there I saw the white man's expression change from stare to puzzlement to fright. He ran his hands over his eyes as if to blot out an image. My girl friend, Beatrice, nudged me. "Daisy!" I did not move. The man jumped up from the bench and walked away, looking back at me. Beatrice asked, "What was all that? Did he say something bad to you?" I didn't answer.

As we were about to leave the store, Beatrice said, "Wait for me, I must speak to the old man." I followed her and stood back as she talked to the "old man." He was an elderly and retired mill worker who was now nearly crippled with arthritis. When the weather was clear, he always sat on the porch and chatted with the mill workers. He knew all the town's gossip. He knew all the children, both white and Negro, by name. He usually brought a lunch in a paper bag

16

which he kept by his side. Out of this he often produced candy for us kids. Needless to say, he was to the children the most popular person in town.

I heard Beatrice tell him there was a new baby at her house. He reached in the bag and gave her a peppermint stick. He held out another for me. When I refused, he said to Bea, "What's wrong with her? She lost her sweet tooth?" Bea repeated after him, "What's the matter with you?"

I started to walk away. "Nothing," I said.

Bea caught up with me. "What's wrong with you, Daisy? You aren't any fun any more!"

"If I want candy, I have some money to buy it," I said. "I don't want anything from white people."

The next day, after school, I asked my adopted mother if she needed anything from the commissary. No, she didn't need anything, but our neighbor wanted me to go to the store for her. I ran all the way.

As I neared the store, I saw the same young white man who had stared at me. He was seated on the same bench. I walked slowly until I reached the steps, then stopped. The man glared at me as if to say, "Look at me all you damned please." I didn't take my eyes off him. Suddenly he leaped to his feet and yelled, "Stop staring at me, you bitch!"

He started toward me. I was too frightened to move. I heard the sharp scraping sound of a chair being pushed back. I turned to see the old man standing, holding onto his chair, watching us both. The man who stared also saw him. He stopped. Then in a thin, weak voice, he muttered: "Go away! Haven't I suffered enough?" He walked slowly away.

I watched his back disappear around the corner. I was no longer afraid, for I knew he was more afraid of me than I was of him. I turned to go into the store, and the old man sank back in his chair.

During the following months I would find some way to get to the commissary at least every other day. By now I had a name for the man on the bench. "Drunken Pig." Each time he seemed a little drunker and a little dirtier than the last. At times he would stare back at me; other times he would pretend that he did not see me. But I could tell from the twitching of his mouth and his uneasy glance that he knew I was there.

One day as I was leaving the store, a little white girl about my own age, with whom I had been friends for a long time, ran up behind me and poked me in the back. "Daisy! Daisy!" When I turned around, she said, "Look, Daisy, I have two pennies. Let's buy some candy and I'll tell you about my vacation."

All my hostility and bitterness must have shown on my face, because she pulled back with a frightened look. I slapped her face. "Don't you ever touch me again! I don't want your penny!"

She put her hands to her cheeks and looked at me in disbelief. I jumped down the store steps and ran away, tears streaming from my eyes. When I reached home, my mother was out. I sat on the front porch, crying and waiting for her. I wondered if I should tell my mother and daddy what had happened. How could I ever make my friend understand why I had struck her? I hardly knew the reason myself.

I wanted badly to go back and tell her I was sorry, and that I didn't really hate her. During our friendship we had often met at the store and shared our pennies. We would have so much fun shopping with our pennies. If I bought winding balls, she would buy peppermint sticks and we would divide them.

How could I explain to her that . . . Suddenly I was afraid. Suppose she went home and told her people that I had hit her? Suppose they came for me or my daddy that night?

I remembered hearing of a white man who went to the home of a Negro family, carrying a wide leather belt, and made the father beat his son to teach him to "respect white folks." The white man's daughter was said to have told the Negro boy, "Get off the walk, nigger, and let me pass." The Negro boy is said to have replied, "You don't own all the sidewalk. There's plenty room for you to pass, and if you think I'm going to get off the sidewalk into the muddy street, you're crazy."

The boy did not attend school after that incident, and the family soon moved away.

When my mother arrived home, I decided not to tell her that I had struck my white friend.

Near Christmas, the weather got very cold. The old pot-bellied stove at the school acted up. Most of the time we sat in class all day with our coats on. One of the boys who worked in the store in the evening with his father told us that the store had put out the Christmas toys on display. I dashed home, then hastened to the store to look at them. I rushed right past Drunken Pig. He was slumped in his usual place on the porch bench. I walked around the store looking at the toys. Three men were leaning on the counter where the dolls were. I was standing behind them, admiring a big colored doll, when the door opened and Drunken Pig came stumbling in. I heard one of the men say, "What's happened to him?"

One of the other men said, "I got an idea what's happened.

You heard about that colored woman they found in the mill-pond a few years ago? I heard he was involved . . . leastwise, he started to drink about then, and he's been getting worse and worse ever since. He's about hit rock bottom. Too bad, 'cause he had a good job at that time."

"If he don't work, how does he buy liquor?" one of the men asked.

"He helps the bootleggers clean out their mash barrels."

I stood motionless, listening. Now that I was sure of what I had suspected, I lost all interest in the doll.

Christmas, the happy, exciting anticipation of the magic hour when Santa Claus would come laden with gifts and goodies, had no real meaning for me that year. Our church was preparing for the annual Christmas pageant, depicting the birth of the Christ Child. One of the church ladies came to see Mother to describe the part I was to play—an angel hovering over the straw crib of the Infant Jesus. "She was *so* pretty in her angel costume last Christmas," the lady cooed. Mother was smiling. She was obviously pleased. To everyone's astonishment. I snapped, *"No!* I won't!"

"What is it?" Mother exclaimed. "What is it, my dear?"

"I don't want to," I cried. "I don't want no part of that play about a dead white doll!"

Mother was shocked. "I won't have that kind of talk!" she protested. "You stop that kind of talk this minute!"

"All the pictures I ever saw of Jesus were white," I screamed. "If Jesus is like the white people, I don't want any part of Him!" I fled from the room, leaving everyone in a state of consternation.

Nothing more was ever said about my appearing in the Christmas play. While my friends and family attended the

Christmas pageant, I spent a lonely evening with my dog and colored doll.

With the coming of spring, I went through the daily routine of school and homework. I had come to enjoy tormenting Drunken Pig. I felt as if I were making him pay for his sin. I also blamed him for the loss of my white girl friend, whom I now missed dreadfully. I remembered how we used to meet at the store and look at magazines and daydream about places we would like to go together. One day we were looking through a magazine and saw a picture of New York, with the Statue of Liberty in the background. How would it be to go there one day, as her seventeen-year-old cousin had done? While we were musing she turned to me and asked, "Do you think it will always be like this? I can't come to your house and you can't come to mine?"

I watched Drunken Pig cringe when he was sober enough to recognize me at the commissary. He sank lower and lower. The old crippled man sitting on the porch was always the silent observer of these encounters. His eyes did not smile as much as they used to. I felt, in a way, that he was suffering along with me and Drunken Pig. The old man had not spoken a word to me since the day I refused his candy.

Spring was everywhere. The trees were budding and people were plowing their gardens. One morning I heard Mother say to my father, "I think we should send Daisy away for a visit with her grandmother. I don't think this town is good for her. She doesn't take an interest in anything around the house any more. I asked her if she wanted her flower garden spaded. She even refused that. All she wants to do is go to the store. I wish I knew what was going on in that mind of hers. I saw the mother of that little white girl Daisy used to play with. She asked me why her little girl and Daisy weren't friends any more. I didn't know what to say to her."

At that point I ran into the room and screamed, "Not now! Please! I can't go now!"

They looked at me, puzzled. Daddy finally said, "All right, darling, if you don't want to go to grandma's you don't have to."

March turned damp and windy and cold, but I continued to make almost daily excursions to the commissary. One afternoon I found Drunken Pig asleep. I came closer and looked down on him. When he did not move, I went into the store and bought a winding ball.

Coming out, I saw some men standing around Drunken Pig. They were saying something to one another. After they left I looked all around. Seeing no one but the old man sitting dozing, a blanket around his shoulders, I walked over to Drunken Pig and shook him lightly. When he did not awaken, I shook him again, harder. He opened his eyes slowly. When he saw me, he closed them again, rubbing his hand across his face. Opening his eyes again, he looked at me as I stood staring down at him. I don't know how long we stayed there, staring at each other. Finally he struggled to his feet. In a low, pleading voice, he said, "In the name of God, leave me alone."

Then he turned, half running, half stumbling, and disappeared in the alley behind the store. I walked home happier than I had been in months; yet I was sad, for as I turned away from him, I saw my white friend standing in the door of the store watching me. I smiled and started toward her.

She smiled and held out a bag that I knew held candy. I got almost to her, then turned and walked away. I suddenly remembered that she was white.

During several days of rainy weather I caught a cold and had to stay in. When my cold was better and the rains had ceased, my mother allowed me to go to the store again. At the commissary the old man was dozing in the sun. Drunken Pig wasn't around. I looked in the store. I then went next door to the post office. I came out and stood waiting. The old man sat there watching me for a while. Finally he said, "Daisy, he won't be back no more."

Hesitantly I walked over to him. "He won't be back? Why not?"

"Because they found him in the alley this morning. That's why. He's dead."

"He can't be dead!" I argued.

"He's better off," the old man said quietly, "and so are you."

I could feel the tears come, and I started to turn away lest he see them. But then I started to sob in earnest, and I soon felt the old man's arm about me, holding me close.

"You're the only one in town to cry over that drunkard," the old man whispered in my ear.

When I stopped crying, he reached into his bag and pulled out a large stick of peppermint. "I've been saving this for you," he said earnestly. "Now go home and try to forget." He loosened his embrace and I went on my way.

I walked home in a daze, clutching the candy, feeling numb all over. At home I placed the candy and the money on the table. I suddenly realized I had forgotten to make Mamma's purchase. I walked out into the yard and sat on the woodpile.

That night I kept wishing I could die. I wanted to follow Drunken Pig to hell—I was sure that was where he had gone. A few nights later, when I had gone to bed, my daddy heard me crying. He came in to comfort me. He sat on a chair next to my bed, then took my hand in his.

"I know you've been unhappy for a long time," he began. "I talked with the old crippled man who sits by the commissary. He told me about that drunk who died, and he said I should send you away. Do you want to tell me what it was about?"

Slowly between sobs I told him about my episodes with Drunken Pig. When I finished, Daddy withdrew his hand, wiped the tears from my cheeks, and told me to go to sleep and forget it.

While I had been carrying on my private vendetta against Drunken Pig, I was almost always engaged in open warfare with the neighborhood adults. I felt they were a lazy, conniving bunch of porch sitters who were always chasing us kids around town on errands for them. I resented their rewarding us with stale pound cake and soggy homemade cookies.

One afternoon, after lugging a gallon of milk six blocks for Mrs. Coleman, I watched her reach for a piece of cake from her red-and-white cake pan.

"Thank you, Daisy, for fetching the milk. I always seem to be so tired these days," she said, handing me my reward.

"Shucks, I get tired, too," I said. "And you are always chasing me all over town and then giving me nothing but that old cake. I don't want it—I've been throwing it in the ditch, anyhow."

"Well, did you ever!" said the shocked Mrs. Coleman. "The nerve! I'll certainly see your mother hears about this!"

It was my last feud with adults. My mother had seen to that.

Mother was a tall, dark-brown woman with a kind face and big brown eyes that sparkled when she laughed. She was very religious and believed every word of the Holy Bible—including that passage, "Spare the rod and spoil the child," which I later learned wasn't in the Bible at all. Of course, it made no difference that it wasn't in the Bible, Mamma believed in it just the same.

I was often clobbered, tanned, switched and made to stand in the corner. The floor in the corner was slightly worn from the shuffling of my feet.

Relegated to my customary place in the corner one day, I was deliberately noisier than usual. I knew Mother had a headache, and I reasoned that if I made a lot of noise, she would shoo me out of the house. Then I heard her say to my father, loudly enough for me to hear, "I think I'll fasten Daisy under the house, instead of making her stand in the corner."

My strategy didn't work, and I quieted down. I remembered all too well the bugs and spiders under the house. And recalling the bugs made me think of an evening when a white friend of my father's stopped by our house. He had a little black and white pig in the back of his car. After a lot of conversation, not to mention the refreshments of the evening, our guest decided to spend the night. We could "sleep him" all right, but what to do with his pig was another question. We tried to bed him down in the chicken house, but the old setting hen would have none of that. I offered to take the pig to bed with me. He was so cute, I thought. But one glance from Mother made me drop the subject.

Our house was boxed in, except for an opening left for the plumber. Daddy was the plumber, and the opening was there so he could fix the one water line leading to the kitchen and to the room with the tin tub. It was finally decided to put the pig under the house, and nail boards over the opening.

I thought maybe Mother would put me under the house and nail the opening fast, as was done with the pig. And maybe she'd even forget to let me come out.

I was a regular tomboy and enjoyed competing with the neighborhood boys. I could climb as high as any of them in the old mulberry tree out back of our house. One day, while showing off, I fell from a tree and landed on broken glass imbedded in the ground. I was afraid to go home—being more afraid of a beating than the bleeding leg. When I got home, Mamma didn't scold me after all. She rushed me to the doctor, who took several stiches in my knee. After that I limited my competition with the boys to the ground.

I had never learned to play marbles, so I decided to pay the neighborhood marble champ a penny a lesson to teach me. He demanded a dime, but he taught me well.

During one of our marble games in my back yard, I won one of the boy's favorite agates, and he wanted it back. When I refused, an argument ensued. Mother came out to check the disturbance, and the blabbermouth told her I had his agate and wouldn't give it back.

"Daisy, give him back his marble!" she shouted at me. "You know you're not supposed to play for keeps! That's gambling and gambling is a sin! Now give him back his marble this instant!"

Of course Daddy sinned every Saturday night with his stud-poker friends. The next morning at breakfast he'd hear Mother admonish, "If you must play that devil's game, the least you could do is go to church and ask the Lord to forgive you."

Daddy always put his winnings on the dresser before going to bed, and Mother always took account of his financial rating before beginning her lecture. If he had won, Daddy could be sure of God's and Mamma's forgiveness. But if he had lost, he would have a stern God and a sterner Mamma to contend with.

One Sunday morning I said, "Daddy, why don't you go to church and ask God to forgive you for a whole month? Then you won't have to go to church every Sunday."

Mother fanned my tail and sent me off to Sunday school. After that I left it to Mamma and God to worry about Daddy's sins.

When the news got around the neighborhood that Mother would make me give back marbles, the whole gang descended on our house.

"Miss Susie," they'd say, "Daisy got our marbles."

Mother made me drag out my shoe box full of marbles. Surprised by the extent of my successes, she gave me an "I'll-take-care-of-you-later" look. Then she turned to the little thieves and told them sweetly, "Now, each one of you go take your own marbles." While they scrambled over the marbles I had won from the other kids, she lectured them on "playing for keeps."

That evening at dinner, Mother blamed Daddy for the whole thing. "Daisy has been playing marbles for keeps!" Mother ranted. She had a shoe box full of marbles she won off the boys. You see what you're doing to your daughter?"

27

Daddy smiled. "Are you really that good?" he asked me.

Before I could answer, Mother snapped, "You stop that kind of talk. Can't you see what you're doing—you and your Saturday night poker games!"

Mother didn't allow me to wait for Sunday. She dragged me off that evening for Wednesday night prayer service, so I could ask God to forgive me for my sins.

The summers of the following years, for the most part, were spent on our farm in eastern Arkansas where my grandmother lived with a brown hound dog, and old gray riding horse, a temperamental milk cow, and pigs fattening for winter meat. Occasionally we would take a trip to other states, or I would be sent to visit friends or relatives of my parents.

I was in my teens. On one of my visits away from home my mother sent for me. My father had been taken to the hospital. When I arrived home, the doctor told me it was just a matter of time. Daddy was gravely ill. The bottom dropped out of my world.

One night Daddy told Mother to go home and get some sleep. "Daisy will stay with me," he assured her.

When Mother and the nurse had left, I stood looking down at his tired dark face against the white of the bed linen. I saw the wrinkles etched deep by a lifetime of struggle, and I saw a stubborn chin and proud high forehead. I started to cry, softly. He opened his eyes. "Don't cry for me, Daisy," he moaned. "I know I'm going to die, but—"

I started to protest, but his upraised hand stopped me. He knew I knew, and to deny it would make meaningless the honesty we'd always held to in our lifelong relationship with each other. He said calmly, "I'll be better off." I knew this was so. He had cancer.

"I haven't much to leave you, Daisy, so come close and listen and remember what I have to say to you."

I drew a chair up close and placed my hand in his.

"You're filled with hatred. Hate can destroy you, Daisy. Don't hate white people just because they're white. If you hate, make it count for something. Hate the humiliations we are living under in the South. Hate the discrimination that eats away at the soul of every black man and woman. Hate the insults hurled at us by white scum—and then try to do something about it, or your hate won't spell a thing."

"I'm listening to every word you say, Daddy, and I'll try to do what you say. But rest—you must rest now."

He closed his eyes and shook his head impatiently. "I'll decide when I need rest."

How I loved this strong man who all his life had not been able to use his strength in the way he wanted to. He was forced to suppress it and hold himself back, bow to the white yoke or be cut down. And now that his life was ebbing, he was trying to draw on that reservoir of unused strength to give me a lasting inheritance.

"Daisy," he resumed, "nothing's going to change all of a sudden, and any Negro speaking out alone will suffer. But more and more will join him, and the blacks, acting together will one day . . ."

His voice grew faint. I held my breath. Starting afresh, he continued haltingly, "I remember the day of your mother's funeral. I went to the post office for the mail. I had on my best dark suit. When I came out of the post office, there were three young white hoodlums standing on the steps. One of them said, 'Look at that dressed-up ape! You live here, boy?'

29

When I didn't answer, two of them blocked my path and the other one said, 'I know what's wrong, he needs something red on!' He picked up a brush from a paint bucket. It was left there by painters who'd been painting the brick foundation around the buildings. He painted a red streak down the back of my coat. Then they walked away, laughing. I stood there with murder in my heart. I could've crushed the life out of him with my bare hands. But I knew if I touched one hair on his head I could be lynched.

"On my way home I met one of the deputy sheriffs. I showed him my coat and told him what had happened. He laughed and said, 'Don't get so upset about a little thing like that. They were just having a little fun. Turpentine will take the paint out of your coat.' "

Daddy stopped talking and closed his eyes. I just sat there, constantly patting his hard knuckles, hoping he would speak again. He did. This time his voice, still distinct, was softer than before but more labored.

"Sometimes," he said, "you know later when you should have died. I ought to have died the day they put the paint on my coat. I should have taken those guys and wrung their necks like chickens. But I wanted to live—for what, I sometimes wonder."

I stopped patting the back of his hand, and he drifted off into a sleep. Looking at him, I sensed he would never awaken. It was now nearly daybreak. When the Catholic Sister came into the room, I greeted her warmly. It was the first time in several years that I had spoken to a white person in a pleasant voice.

I walked out into the silent streets. The grass, heavy with dew, caught the sun's early rays. In most of the yards flowers still bloomed, and in many, red roses. I thought of another

30

such morning years ago, and of the red rose I couldn't bear to pick. I knew like that rose which clung to its branch in a last, flaming farewell, my father would die before the end of the day. I did not cry now for I realized that he was at peace with himself for the first time in years.

As I walked along the street taking in the freshness of the early morning air, I knew that as surely as my father was dying, I was undergoing a rebirth. My father had passed on to me a priceless heritage—one that was to sustain me throughout the years to come.

CHAPTER III

ACROSS MY DESK

One day when I was fifteen years old, a tall, slender, soft-spoken insurance agent came to visit my father, who had been referred to him as a likely prospect. My father purchased a family policy. And for the next three years, even though his territory took in a sizable section of the state, L. C. Bates was a frequent visitor at our home.

He and my father became fast friends during those years. L. C. would bring Dad newspapers and magazines that could not be purchased in our home town, a box of candy for Mother, and I could always be sure of a special gift, such as a string of simulated pearls or a bracelet. Sometimes he would invite the three of us to the local movies.

One such evening L. C. held my hand in the dark theater and I was thrilled, for I had grown to love and respect him during his visits. That evening I paid little attention to the movie for I decided, then and there, that I would one day marry him. I didn't reveal my plans to L. C.—or to my family. Daddy had often declared that a girl should not consider marriage until she could cook and sew. And I could do neither.

However, L. C. soon became aware of my feelings for him. Shortly after my father's death he proposed marriage and I readily accepted.

L. C. was born in Mississippi. When he graduated from the public schools of his home county, he went to Wilberforce College in Ohio, where he majored in journalism. He worked for three years on a newspaper in Colorado, then joined the staff of the *Kansas City Call* in Missouri. These were the years of the great depression of the thirties. The life of a struggling Negro newspaper was most insecure, let alone the position of a young inexperienced reporter. L. C. lost his job. He then turned to selling insurance.

After our marriage we settled in Little Rock. It soon became evident that L. C., although a successful insurance man, much preferred newspaper work. His urge to go back to that business was irresistible. He reasoned, "If I own the paper, I won't lose my job." Together we decided to lease the newspaper plant of a struggling church paper and invest our savings in a weekly newspaper, the *State Press*. The decision was not made lightly. I held out, in fact, for several weeks against the venture, realizing that such a project required possibly more money and effort than the two of us had to give.

The lifeblood of any newspaper is its advertising revenue.

Unless we could be assured of some support from the utilities, the national advertisers, the local department stores, and the like, our newspaper might not survive more than a few months.

L. C. and I decided to gamble on the newspaper's success. We thought it was a gamble worth taking. Our decision was based on the conviction that a newspaper was needed to carry on the fight for Negro rights as nothing else can. If we could get advertisers to support a crusading paper, all well and good. If not—well, that was part of the gamble.

In its first months the *State Press* grew in circulation to a healthy ten thousand—half the total readership it was to achieve at its peak. And as its circulation grew, so did its advertising revenue. Slowly but surely the *State Press* became a voice to be reckoned with not only among its Negro readers but in the white communities in key sections of the state.

There was not lack of causes for which to crusade. Police brutality was rampant. Negroes were beaten unmercifully by the city police of Little Rock at the slightest provocation. This seemed the most urgent cause to which we should devote our first crusade.

The campaign against police brutality went on relentlessly but fruitlessly. It wasn't until World War II was declared that a series of local events enabled us to make a real breakthrough.

With the onset of the war the businessmen in Little Rock started a movement to get nearby Camp Robinson reopened. Their efforts were successful, and thousands of soldiers of all races, with lots of spending money, were eventually sent to the camp. But with the huge increase in business profits came a huge increase in police brutality to Negroes. The city police had a field day beating the Negro soldiers who came into town on weekend passes and who ran afoul of the law. The *State Press* printed stories. Citizens protested. Nothing happened.

Army officials meanwhile showed no interest in such purely "civilian" affairs. After all, the local police had a long record of beating Negroes. So why become disturbed because a few Northern soldiers complained about being beaten?

On March 2, 1942, a Sunday afternoon, the thing we had feared most happened—a city policeman cold-bloodedly shot to death a Negro soldier. He was Sergeant Thomas P. Foster, one of the most popular and respected soldiers on the post. When I arrived at the scene to cover the story for my newspaper, hundreds of citizens had already gathered in silence. Together we watched the police conduct their "investigation." The shrill siren of the ambulance broke the silence as it made its way through the crowded street. People stood looking in the direction of the ambulance as it carried away the bullet-ridden body of Sergeant Foster.

A Negro soldier standing next to me was crying openly. He threw his neatly pressed Army cap on the ground and stamped on it with the irreverence born of anger and bitterness. "Why should we go over there and fight? These are the sons of bitches we should be fighting!" His words, directed at no one in particular, were nevertheless understood by the handful of people who heard them. I looked down at the cap now lying shapeless on the ground. I knew that the cap represented every white person who had ever called him "nigger" —all the suppressed emotion of a lifetime of oppression.

Slowly the crowd began to disperse, leaving the soldier standing alone, still stamping his cap. Soon a Negro sergeant came over, took him by the arm, and led him gently to the bus for Camp Robinson.

With my notebook in hand I hurried back to the office of the *State Press.* There later appeared the following story:

CITY PATROLMAN SHOOTS NEGRO SOLDIER
Body Riddled While Lying on Ground

One of the most bestial murders in the annals of Little Rock occurred Sunday afternoon at 5:45 o'clock at Ninth and Gaines Streets, in front of hundreds of onlookers, when Patrolman A. J. Hay shot and mortally wounded Sergeant Thomas P. Foster, member of Company D, 92nd Engineers, stationed at Camp Robinson.... When Sgt. Foster asked the Military Police why they had Pvt. Albert Glover...in custody, City Policeman Hay interfered and struck Sgt. Foster with his night stick. A scuffle ensued, whereupon Policeman Hay threw Sgt. Foster to the ground and then fired five shots from his pistol into his prostrate body. Sgt. Foster died in the University Hospital five hours later....

The story proved upsetting to the white community, particularly to the downtown stores that relied heavily on the soldier trade. The tradesmen were afraid that the camp would be closed and their booming source of business would suddenly disappear.

But the outraged Negro community would not respond to the hush-hush pleadings of the businessmen who wished to gloss over the brutality. Meetings were called by Negro civic leaders to protest the wanton slaying of Sergeant Foster. The *State Press,* in spite of threats from local businessmen, continued its crusade against the murder.

Five days after Sergeant Foster was slain, all the downtown stores canceled their advertising in the *State Press.* The newspaper suffered its first crippling blow in the struggle for human rights and dignity.

The future of the *State Press* looked bleak. Our assets and liabilities shaped up roughly as follows: ten thousand readers, one twenty-dollar-a-month classified ad, a five-year lease on the printing plant, a monstrous flat-bed press that groaned and screeched with each revolution, and an eccentric folding machine that would fold about half of the papers and then freeze, making it necessary to fold the rest of the press run by hand.

The picture was discouraging. So much so that I was tempted to pack up and leave Little Rock. The paper was nearly a year old and it had shown a profit almost from the first issue. But in spite of its ten thousand readers, the advertisers' boycott made it impossible to purchase new machinery that would improve the newspaper operation. "Let's face it," I told L. C. "We can't operate without advertisers. Let's quit now while we still have train fare."

"Things aren't that bad, Daisy," he said with a smile. "We still have a reserve in the *State Press* account, and, of course, our savings."

"And after that's gone, then what?" I asked.

"We'll try taking the paper to the people," L. C. said. "We won't get rich but at least we'll be able to make a living. And what's more important we'll be able to publish a free and independent paper."

We decided to stick to our guns. L. C. and I went to work from twelve to eighteen hours a day in order to keep our paper going. We put on an all-out campaign against police brutality, and this time we struck a responsive note among those who had long had to suffer in silence and shame from the crude injustice of the police. The Negroes supposedly fighting a war in the name of freedom had through our paper found a voice to express their feelings. Our circulation began to climb rapidly, reaching twenty thousand in a few months, and as it continued to climb we were able to attract a fairly profitable advertising clientele among the small, independent off-Main Street merchants who catered to our kind of readers.

From this beginning the *State Press* expanded its crusading role on an ever widening front. It fought to free Negroes from muddy, filthy streets, slum housing, menial jobs, and injustice in the courtrooms. In time, certain changes came over Little Rock. Small, integrated organizations working for the advancement of the Little Rock community took heart and became bolder. They began to exert political and economic pressure against violations of fundamental rights guaranteed all Americans under the Constitution. They refused to be intimidated, as in the past, by threats of retaliation. Instances of police brutality became less frequent, and when they did occur their perpetrators could not expect to get off with only a mild reprimand. Negro police replaced white police in the Negro business section. Eventually such a profound change was effected that Little Rock actually began to gain a reputation as a liberal southern city.

July 8, 1945, was a red-letter day for the *State Press*. In my white coveralls I stood with L. C. in the new home of the *State Press* watching the unloading of our new printing equipment. Friends sent flowers. Someone brought a bottle of champagne. We celebrated! The *State Press* was about to embark upon a new life.

Shortly after we founded the *State Press*, I enrolled at Shorter College, taking courses in Business Administration, Public Relations, and other subjects related to the newspaper field.

I had always liked flying. So when Milton Crenchaw, the son of the Reverend J. C. Crenchaw, President of the local NAACP branch, came home from the war and operated a flight school in connection with Philander Smith College, I was among the first to enroll. It turned out that I was the only woman in the class. I had just about acquired enough time in the air to qualify for my license when my insurance agent learned that I was taking flying lessons. He thereupon revised my insurance rates upward. The new premiums were so astronomical that they put an end to my flight career.

In March, 1946, L. C. went off on a much-needed vacation. I was temporarily the proud editor-in-chief, responsible for getting the paper out all on my own. A few days after L. C. left, I was the first reporter to arrive on a murder scene to cover the story. A woman had slain her husband and was placed in the city jail. There the reporters had tried to interview her, but she refused to talk to them. I decided to try. I used the sympathetic approach. When I entered her cell, I said, "You poor dear, I'm sure he must have been a brute."

"You're right. He was just no damn good. He was the kind who stayed out all hours and then beat you up when he came home."

"Yes, I know," I said feelingly.

"You do? You mean Mr. Bates beats you, too?"

"Of course," I said.

"You poor thing. I'll tell you how to stop him."

Suddenly I began to picture what L. C. would say if he could overhear me ruining his reputation. The mere thought amused me to tears. Real tears. Obviously convinced that I was crying because of my sad plight, she began to cry herself. When I left her cell about a half hour later, I remarked, "If there's anything I can do, please let me know."

"Thanks, honey," she called through the bars, "just stop that man from beating you. You're too little."

While L. C. was still on vacation I covered a story of another kind. Oil workers, members of the CIO, were on strike at the Southern Cotton Oil Mill, about a mile from the *State Press* office. There were rotating shifts of four men picketing the plant. In the course of events, Walter Campbell, a picket, was killed while on the picket line by Otha Williams, who had been hired to take the place of a striking worker. The other pickets, Roy Cole, Jesse Bean, and Louis Jones, were arrested along with Williams.

The wheels of justice, Arkansas style, immediately began turning. Otha Williams was acquitted of the murder charge, and the three union pickets were found guilty of violating the Arkansas "Right-to-Work" law and were sentenced to a year's imprisonment. The law contains an antiviolence clause that prohibits violence on a picket line. If any violence occurs on a picket line, any striker present can be found guilty.

The *State Press* felt this was a grave miscarriage of justice, and it was prepared to say just that. My story was fresh out of the typewriter when L. C. returned from his vacation. He read the story. "Daisy," he cautioned, "this is a pretty strong story. Do you realize that Judge Auten is one of the most powerful men in the state?"

"That may be," I said, "but you and I know that the real intent of this law is to destroy organized labor in Arkansas."

L. C. wrote the headline for my story, which appeared in the *State Press* on March 29, 1946:

FTA STRIKERS SENTENCED TO PEN
BY A HAND-PICKED JURY

Three strikers, who by all observation were guilty of no greater crime than walking on a picket line, were sentenced to one year in the penitentiary yesterday by a "hand-picked" jury, while a scab who killed a striker is free.

The prosecution was hard pressed to make a case until Judge Lawrence C. Auten instructed the jury that the pickets could be found guilty if they aided or assisted, or just stood idly by while violence occurred.

Motions to quash the indictments were overruled by the judge. These motions included protests to the fact that there were no Negroes on the jury in accordance with the law.

Appeal bond was fixed at $2,500 each. The usual bond in such cases is $1,000.

Shortly after my story appeared, two Pulaski County Police Sheriffs came to our home and knocked at the door. "We have a warrant for your arrests," one said, as he handed us the summons. We were told to read it. It stated: "You are commanded to take L. C. Bates and Mrs. L. Christopher Bates, City Editors of the *Arkansas State Press* and them safely keep so that they be and appear before the first division circuit court of Pulaski County, Arkansas, on the 29th day of April, at 9:30 A.M. to answer the people of Arkansas for contempt of court . . ."

We were booked, fingerprinted, and photographed with our numbers. We were then allowed to post bond. We called several lawyers, some of whom had represented us in the past. But they were all "too busy" or had important business out of the city. We were finally able to secure the services of the two CIO lawyers, Elmer Schoggen and Ross Robley, who were representing the strikers at the Southern Cotton Oil Mill.

When we returned from jail, to the *State Press* office, our office secretary, Pauline Weaver, said: "Mr. Bates, I don't think you can afford to take another vacation after this."

"You're right," L. C. shot back. "In thirty days, Daisy has not only made me a wife beater, but she has also accused one of the state's biggest judges of dishonesty on the bench, questioned the honesty of the jury commissioners and jury panels, and attacked the integrity of the entire court and its administration of justice."

In court, on April 29, Judge Auten served as judge and jury for the hearing. He explained that jury commissioners, petit and grand jury panels, are integral parts of the court. He further stated: "The article in the *State Press* implied that the entire court was dishonest and carried an implication that these men [Negro strikers] were railroaded to the penitentiary."

Our attorney, Schoggen, argued that the jury trying the strikers was indeed hand-picked. "It was our conception and it is still our conception," he pleaded, "that many persons by training and environment are not qualified to try Negro strikers."

Judge Auten sentenced L. C. and me to ten days in prison and $100 fine. Appeal bond was denied by the court on the grounds that a contempt conviction was not appealable. We were taken to the county jail. As I approached the cell, I recognized the woman I had interviewed about three weeks earlier, who had killed her husband. We were now to be cellmates. I turned to the jailer and whispered, "Do you have another cell you can put me in?"

"No," he answered roughly, "this is the only one we have. Get in there! I don't have all day!"

My cellmate watched the jailer until he disappeared. "He's

a no-good bastard," she confided. She then smiled and said soothingly, "Don't be so scared, honey. It ain't that bad in here. Anyway, the people out there ain't gonna let you stay in here no ten days. My second husband use to say them CIO lawyers are the smartest there is. They'll get you out."

Seven hours later we were released on a $500 cash bond each on the order of Arkansas Supreme Court Justice Griffin Smith, who granted a supersedeas and a writ of certiorari under which our case would be reviewed by the Arkansas Supreme Court. On November 11, 1946, the Arkansas State Supreme Court ordered the judgment quashed, with directions to dismiss the actions. Justice Smith stated in his opinion: "We know of no rule of law permitting jail sentences and contempt fines merely because a newspaper thinks some judge mistakenly stated the law. Such comment does not create a present danger to the administration of justice.

> When on September 7, 1874, certain distinguished gentlemen subscribed to the proposition set out as Art. II, Sec. 6 of the [State] Constitution, they were not expressing new thought, but reasserted an opinion then common among men: "The liberty of the press shall forever remain inviolate. The free communication of thoughts and opinion is one of the invaluable rights of man; and all persons may freely write and publish their sentiments on all subjects, being responsible for the abuse of such right."
>
> A distinction might be drawn between writing and publishing one's "sentiments," as the term is used in the Constitution, and in printing diatribes where public institutions charged with the administration of justice are singled out. Any arbitrary line we might attempt to draw would be subject to restrictions . . .

World War II ended. Negro soldiers came marching home shortly after V-J Day, September 2, 1945, with a new-found dignity gained from the knowledge that they had served their country well. Many had been wounded fighting for democracy in far-off battlefields. Some proudly displayed silver stars, bronze stars, purple hearts, and other decorations earned for courageous action in combat. Their joy at being home, of again seeing their loved ones, was overshadowed only by the memory of the lonely graves of buddies in foreign fields, and of the deadly mushroom clouds that hung over Hiroshima and Nagasaki after America exploded the atomic bomb on August 6, 1945.

After the welcomes and the tributes and citations for bravery were made, the Negro soldiers, particularly those in the South, brought a new spirit of militancy, born of combat, to the fight for equality.

In January, 1946, over one hundred Negro World War II veterans marched on the courthouse in Birmingham, Alabama, to register to vote. They were turned down by a white supremacy hoax that they were unable satisfactorily to "interpret the United States Constitution," although Alabama's law demands only that voters be able to read and write. In other parts of the South, many returning Negro servicemen were the first to register and vote since Reconstruction days.

I remember the case of one returning veteran in Little Rock, a young Army captain, recently discharged. He visited me at the *State Press* office one afternoon.

"Being home isn't as pleasant as I had thought," said the captain. "For the past four years, while in the Army, I was treated as a man. I was judged and respected on the basis of character and ability, not color. Today I walked into a man's store on Main Street and was greeted with 'What do you want, boy?' I looked at the clerk, turned and walked out, After leaving the store, I passed a restaurant. Hungry and angry, without thinking, I entered. As I approached a table, I suddenly became aware of a screaming silence prevailing in the room. I stood at the table with my hand on a chair. As I looked around the room, the cold raw hatred that I saw in the eyes of the waitresses and customers stabbed more deadly and with greater pain than the fragments of the shell that injured my leg in Germany. I stood there for a moment, looking at their faces distorted with hate, thinking of the tribute America paid to *dead* heroes, black and white, and I said, 'Pardon me,' and walked out."

My heart went out to this young man, slumped in the chair opposite my desk. His colorful war decorations were pinned on his chest, and silver bars on his shoulders glistened in the overhead light.

"I'm leaving the South," he ended resignedly. "There must be some place in America where a Negro can be a man."

During the months that followed, hundreds of news items crossed my desk recounting the incredible brutalities committed against Negro veterans by white Americans. Proud men returning from war, victorious defenders of their country, were deprived of their dignity and relegated to the status of second-class citizens. The least altercation between Negro soldier and white civilian was used as an opportunity to "put the Nigras in line." The *State Press* was to carry column after column of some of the worst offenses ever committed against any people, white or Negro. One such story:

On February 12, 1946, Isaac Woodard, Jr., a twenty-seven-year-old veteran of four years' service and recipient of a battle star, had his eyes gouged out in Batesburg, South Carolina, by the town's chief of police. It happened less than five hours after his discharge from the Army.

Woodard checked out of Camp Gordon, Georgia, at 5:30 P.M. At 8:30 P.M. he caught a bus from Atlanta, Georgia, for Winnsboro, South Carolina. He was to meet his wife there and continue on to New York City for a reunion with his parents.

About one hour out of Atlanta, the driver stopped at a bus stop, a combination filling station and grocery store. Woodard asked the driver if he would have time to go to the rest room. The driver said no, and cursed Woodard. Woodard cursed him back. The driver then told him to go ahead, but to hurry back. Half an hour later the bus stopped at Batesburg, South Carolina. The driver called the police. An officer showed up and ordered Woodard off the bus for creating a disturbance. Woodard tried to explain to the officer that he had done nothing, but was immediately struck in the face with a billy and arrested.

En route to jail the policeman asked Woodard if he had been discharged from the service. Woodard said "Yes." The policeman started to beat him again. "You say, 'yes, *sir*'," he demanded.

In jail Woodard was beaten again. This time he was bashed repeatedly in the eyes with a billy. The next morning, when told to prepare to go before the judge, Woodard told the policeman that he could not see. The policeman led him to a washbasin and told him he would feel better after washing his face. Then he was led into the courtroom, where he was fined fifty dollars for "disturbing the peace."

The beating left Isaac Woodard, Jr., blinded for life.

These and other atrocities created in the veteran a stubborn determination to oppose a segregated system that permitted injustices by policemen who were rarely punished but often promoted. This determination was manifested in many ways. Among them was membership in the National Association for the Advancement of Colored People. Enlistment in this and other civil rights organizations swelled to an all-time high.

From our first days in Little Rock we were members of the local branch of the NAACP. The branch was headed by the late Reverend W. Marcus Taylor. In all the years of his leadership, he was admired for his wisdom and breadth of understanding. He was a strikingly tall, elderly man, handsome and well educated. He came to my office at the *State Press* one day to discuss the association's growth in the state. He foresaw the oncoming struggles and believed they would require young, fresh leadership. At that time I was co-chairman of the State Conference's Committee for Fair Employment Practices (F.E.P.C.). Mr. Taylor thought I should be the person to head the State Conference of NAACP branches. With no opposition I was elected president of the Arkansas State Conference of NAACP branches in 1952.

Throughout the South a rash of lawsuits was filed attacking segregation in public education. Under the leadership of Thurgood Marshall, NAACP attorneys consolidated four of these suits. These ultimately led to the historic decision of May 17, 1954, when the United States Supreme Court declared segregation in public education to be unconstitutional. It ruled that all school segregation laws were invalid and that therefore "all provisions of federal, state or local law requiring or permitting such discrimination must yield to this principle."

To the nation's Negroes the Supreme Court decision meant that the time for delay, evasion, or procrastination was past. It meant that whatever difficulties in according Negro children their constitutional rights, it was nevertheless clear that school boards must seek a solution to that question in accordance with the law of the land.

Several school boards immediately announced plans for desegregation. Only five days after the Supreme Court decision, Fayetteville, Arkansas, announced that six Negro high-school students who had been forced to attend a school sixty miles from their homes would be admitted to the local high school in August, 1954.

The school board in Charleston, Arkansas, another small community, also announced it would integrate the eleven Negro students into its public school system in the fall. Similar announcements were issued by the Catholic schools in Fort Smith and Paris, declaring their intentions to admit Negro Catholic students for the first time.

Along with most daily newspapers in the United States, the *State Press* shared the exultation of civic and religious organizations in the Supreme Court's ruling. While politicians and racists in the southern states advocated open defiance of the Court's decision, the *State Press* took heart in the pledge of the Governor, Francis A. Cherry, that "Arkansas would obey the law."

The decision came during the height of the campaign for Governor; and Governor Cherry, who was seeking re-election to a second term, stated that integration should not be made an issue in the campaign. His political opponent, Orval Eugene Faubus, saw a political advantage in striking a different pose. In a formal statement he declared:

> It is evident to me that Arkansas is not ready for a complete and sudden mixing of the races in the public schools and that any attempt to solve this problem by pressure or

mandatory methods will jeopardize, in many communities, the good relations which exist between whites and Negroes.

In my opinion, de-segregation is the No. 1 issue in this gubernatorial campaign and I am therefore making my position clear at the outset with the expressed hope that this issue does not become a temptation to acts and declarations of demagoguery on the part of those who might seek to play upon racial prejudice for selfish ends or, as in the case of communism, to create ill will between whites and Negroes and disrupt this country.

Faubus was elected and assumed office in January, 1955.

Ten days after the Supreme Court decision was handed down, the Little Rock School Board announced a complicated plan for desegregating the schools. Its plan was to be carried out in three phases.

First phase: Integration should begin at the senior high school level (Grades 10-12).

Second phase: Following successful integration at the senior high school level, it should then be started in the junior high schools (Grades 7-9).

Third phase: After successful integration in junior and senior high schools, it should be started in elementary schools (Grades 1-6).

Early in 1955 the Arkansas State Board of Education announced that its seven state colleges would be open in the fall to Negro undergraduate students. The *State Press* noted at that time that the impact of desegregation taking place in these widely separated communities without any violence

Note: The first phase was intended to become effective in the school year 1957-58.

had been cushioned by the fact that Negroes had been attending the Graduate School of the University of Arkansas since 1948.

In the summer of 1955 the community of Hoxie, located 138 miles from Little Rock, faced a crisis. There were fourteen Negro families among the population of 1,284. Nine Negro families had children who attended the Hoxie elementary and high schools. These were segregated schools.

A report to the NAACP on the Negro elementary school gave the following information:

"The school is located two blocks from the sewerage line. Outdoor toilets, woodburning stove, no janitor. Children perform janitorial work. Broken windows, leaking roof. During rainy weather children must wear boots to school in order to get in. All elementary grades housed under one roof with one teacher. Children number approximately twenty-seven."

The crisis arose over the fact that the Hoxie School Board was without sufficient funds to operate a dual school system. On this basis the board decided to integrate the school. Negro parents were advised to send their children to a newer "white" school with adequate facilities and room to absorb the Negro children.

The integration process proceeded smoothly. Negro and white children played and attended classes together without incident. No one could have foreseen that Hoxie would become the forerunner of a series of violent and bitter battles that culminated in the tragic Little Rock disorders.

It began with a meeting of approximately two hundred persons on August 3, 1955. Called together by white racists, they met at the Hoxie City Hall where they adopted a resolution demanding a return to the segregated system. White parents were encouraged to withdraw their children from the school as long as the Negro children remained.

Negro parents were subjected to threats and intimidation, and were even called upon to put their names to a petition demanding the return to the segregated school system. The Negro parents stood firm in their determination to abide by the school board decision to integrate the school.

It is to the everlasting credit of the Hoxie School Board that it refused to yield to racist leaders whose foul tactics to achieve their goal were beginning to have a serious effect on the community's children, both Negro and white.

The school board decided to seek relief in the Federal Court, invoking for the first time the ruling of the Supreme Court of the year before. Now the Federal Court issued an injunction requiring the segregationists to cease their interference with the integration of the Hoxie elementary school. The injunction laid down an important precedent in the larger battles to come.

Curiously, Governor Faubus did not interfere with school districts that had taken steps toward integration. Certainly he must have had advance knowledge of the announcement by the State Board of Education that state colleges would admit Negro undergraduates in the fall term of 1955.

Virgil T. Blossom, superintendent of the Little Rock School District, spent two precious years expounding the virtues of the Little Rock plan for desegregating the schools. However, the plan, having taken many twists and turns, still remained vague and indecisive. Many Negro parents became convinced that Superintendent Blossom was more interested in appeasing the segregationists by advocating that only a limited number of Negroes be admitted than in complying with the Supreme Court's decision. The only assurance Negroes had that the school board would put the highly publicized plan into effect in the foreseeable future was the word of the school board. But years of bitter and tragic experience had taught the Negro that the word of the Southern white man meant very little when it came to granting the Negro his constitutional rights.

About the Little Rock integration plan, Negro parents felt that the phrase "may start in 1957" was especially vague and left them no alternative except to go into court. The parents appealed to the Arkansas State Conference of the National Association for the Advancement of Colored People to represent them.

In the spring of 1956 State Chairman of the NAACP Legal Defense Committee, Wiley Branton, and U. Simpson Tate, regional attorney for the NAACP, filed suit in Federal Court against the Little Rock School District on behalf of thirty-three Negro parents for immediate integration to start in grades one to twelve.

Federal Judge John E. Miller ruled in favor of the school board. He decided that the board had acted in good faith in scheduling its integration plan to start the following year, in September, 1957.

The NAACP attorneys next appealed this decision to the Eighth Circuit Court of Appeals. The Court of Appeals upheld the lower court, but in doing so it handed down a further ruling which was to have far-reaching effects on the integration program and on Little Rock itself. For, in addition to ordering the school board to put its plan into effect as of September, 1957, it ruled that the District Federal Court retain jurisdiction of the case for the purpose of entering such further orders as might be necessary. Even though the NAACP attorneys failed in their attempt to get a court decision ordering *immediate* integration in all grades, the plaintiffs felt confident that the school board, now under court order, would surely have to integrate the schools of Little Rock.

It wasn't until the spring of 1957, during the legislative session, when four pro-segregation bills were introduced, that we realized Governor Faubus was yielding to the pressure of the segregationists. Obviously the bills were introduced with his support.

House Bill No. 322 provided for the creation of a State Sovereignty Commission with many duties, the first of which would be to "perform any and all acts and things deemed necessary" to protect the sovereignty of Arkansas and other states from encroachments by the Federal Government. The bill gave the commission authority to resist the United States Supreme Court decision against segregation in public schools.

House Bill No. 323 made attendance not compulsory in integrated schools.

House Bill No. 324 required persons and organizations engaged in certain activities to register with the State and make regular reports of their income and expenses. This apparently would apply to the National Association for the Advancement of Colored People, in particular.

House Bill No. 325 allowed school boards to use school funds to hire lawyers for integration suits.

The four bills passed the House of Representatives without much debate by a vote of eighty-eight to one. The *State*

Press urged that efforts now be concentrated on the Senate to defeat the bills. The Senate Constitutional Amendment Committee agreed to hold a public hearing.

The meeting was held on February 18, in the House of Representatives. The *State Press* reported it to be one of the largest public hearings in recent times. Nine hundred citizens, the majority of whom were against the passage of the bills, filled the chambers. I sat in the gallery listening to speakers representing church groups and organized labor as they made fervent pleas against passage of the bills. My stories in the *State Press* summarized their remarks:

Rabbi Ira E. Sanders of Temple B'Nai Israel, in Little Rock, warned that "all four bills are concerned with circumventing the legal authority of the Supreme Court and the moral law of God. If they are adopted, it will mean a loss of industry and this would be morally just opprobrium for the State."

Odell Smith of Little Rock, President of the Arkansas State Federation of Labor, asserted that organized labor was opposed to the bills because they were "more in harmony with the principles of Communist and Fascist governments" than with democratic government.

The Reverend W. L. Miller, Jr., of Rogers, President of the Arkansas State Convention of Christian Churches, declared that if the bills passed he could "foresee only dark days of inquisition ahead." He added that "the bills would set up a secret police with undefined powers and that could only mean the loss of our freedom."

The only Negro who spoke was Rev. Roland S. Smith, pastor of the First Baptist Church of Little Rock. He delivered the most impassioned speech of the session. He noted that Negroes had been "separate but equal" for more than sixty years, during which time they had demonstrated love and loyalty for the United States. He said he thanked God that he was an American citizen, and that a faith in God would bring justice and righteousness between the races. "We have nothing to fear but fear itself," he concluded.

Among those speaking for the passage of the bill was its author, R. B. McCulloch of Forrest City, an attorney. He pointed out that the portion of the measure that most persons were objecting to was taken "word for word" from a bill now before the United States Senate.

Former Governor Ben T. Laney, of Altheimer, maintained that "the issue is whether we shall stand back and take the Supreme Court decision with all its implications and not raise our voice against it."

Ben Shaver of Wynne, former Attorney General, closed the argument for supporters of the segregation bills. "You can't turn back history and you can't turn it forward instantly," he said. He added that the bills were designed to delay integration to "let people settle down, and face the matter realistically."

Following the public hearing, NAACP representatives throughout the State visited their senators in an effort to defeat the bills. I was a member of a Pulaski County delegation of business and professional people who visited the Governor in an attempt to get him to use his influence to help defeat the bills.

This was my first formal meeting with the Governor. He was very gracious. But he expressed the opinion that the bills would not infringe upon the rights of any individual or organization. He explained that, as the head of the NAACP in Arkansas, I would only have to submit to the proper authorities a list of the organization's members and a periodical financial statement.

Despite the protest of thousands of citizens, the bills were passed. Thus the machinery was set in motion under which the authorities could jail, intimidate, and coerce Negro and white citizens who dared to speak out against injustices. The new laws gave the White Citizens Council, the Ku Klux Klan, and other such organizations additional legal weapons to bolster their hate campaigns.

Events moved swiftly after that. The White Citizens Councils evidently learned from their scrimmage in Hoxie that if their efforts were to succeed, stronger measures must now be taken against the Negroes as well as those whites who advocated school integration.

As I have already stated, the first phase of the Little Rock School Board integration plan was scheduled to begin September 4 at Central High School. In spite of the strong opposition that had been voiced by the segregationists, most Little Rock citizens did not expect any serious trouble; and they were unprepared for the series of events that developed so rapidly during the last two weeks of August.

On August 27, five days after the rock came crashing through my living-room window, Mrs. Clyde A. Thomason filed suit in Chancery Court seeking a temporary injunction against school integration. Mrs. Thomason was a member of a newly organized segregationist group which called itself the Mothers League of Little Rock Central High School. Ironically, only a handful of the League's members had children who attended Central.

The suit was heard two days later, on August 29, before

56

Judge Murray O. Reed. Mrs. Thomason testified she had been told that the mothers were terrified to send their children to Central because of a rumor that the white and Negro youths were forming gangs and some of them were armed with guns and knives.

Mrs. Thomason's surprise witness was Governor Faubus. He testified that he personally knew that revolvers had been taken from Negro and white pupils. However, neither Mrs. Thomason nor Governor Faubus revealed the source of their information to the court.

At the end of the hearing Judge Reed granted the injunction against integration.

After the hearing that day reporters made a check of all the stores and pawnshops where guns and knives could easily be purchased by teen-agers but they could find nothing to substantiate the charges of the Governor and Mrs. Thomason.

That night the segregationists celebrated. They drove by our home, blowing their horns and yelling: "Daisy! Daisy! Did you hear the news? The coons won't be going to Central!"

The next day Wiley Branton, a local NAACP attorney, and Thurgood Marshall, special counsel of the NAACP, went before Federal Judge Ronald N. Davies with a petition. Judge Davies, who had been temporarily assigned from North Dakota to the Little Rock District, then handed down a decision overruling the Chancery Court and ordering the school board to proceed with immediate integration.

Meanwhile, the hate campaigns sponsored by the Capital Citizens Council, the White Citizens Council, and the Ku Klux Klan were gathering momentum. Speakers from Mississippi and Louisiana appeared before the Capital Citizens Council and advocated "bloodshed if necessary" to keep the

57

Negro children out of the so-called "white schools." Everywhere in Little Rock there were rumors that segregationist forces from hard-core states, the so-called "solid South," were organizing for a fight to the finish against integregation in public education. Little Rock was to be the battleground.

CHAPTER IV

GOVERNOR FAUBUS
ROUSES THE MOB

IT WAS Labor Day, September 2, 1957. The nine pupils who had been selected by the school authorities to enter Central High School—Carlotta Walls, Jefferson Thomas, Elizabeth Eckford, Thelma Mothershed, Melba Pattillo, Ernest Green, Terrance Roberts, Gloria Ray, and Minnijean Brown—were enjoying the last day of their summer vacation. Some of them were picnicking, others swimming, playing tennis, or just visiting with friends and relatives. About mid-afternoon young Jefferson Thomas was on his way home from the pool and stopped at my house for a brief visit. While Jeff was raiding the refrigerator, a news flash came over the radio that the Governor would address the citizens of Arkansas that night.

"I wonder what he's going to talk about," said Jeff. The youngster then turned to me and asked, "Is there anything they can do—now that they lost in court? Is there any way they can stop us from entering Central tomorrow morning?"

"I don't think so," I said.

About seven o'clock that night a local newspaper reporter rang my doorbell. "Mrs. Bates, do you know that national guardsmen are surrounding Central High?"

L. C. and I stared at him incredulously for a moment. A friend who was visiting us volunteered to guard the house while we drove out to Central. L. C. gave him the shotgun. We jumped into our car and drove to Central High. We parked a half block from the school. Under the street lights stretched a long line of brown Army trucks with canvas tops. Men in full battle dress—helmets, boots, and bayonets—were piling out of the trucks and lining up in front of the school.

As we watched, L. C. switched on the car radio. A newscaster was saying, "National guardsmen are surrounding Central High School. No one is certain what this means. Governor Faubus will speak later this evening."

Ahead of us we could see reporters rushing up trying to talk to the soldiers. However, it soon became clear that the guardsmen were under orders to say nothing. They remained silent.

The whole scene was incredible. "Let's go back home and hear Faubus!" I suggested.

The phone was ringing as we pulled into our driveway. An excited friend wanted to know what it all meant, what was going to happen. All I could offer was, "Listen to Faubus."

60

As soon as I put down the receiver, the phone rang again. This time it was the father of one of the children. "What's going on, Daisy? What's going to happen?" All I could do was to give him the same answer.

On television, Governor Faubus creates almost the same impression he does in person. He customarily wears a dark suit, white shirt, and dark tie. He is a big man physically, and affects a big man's easy congeniality. He specializes in the folksy manner, fixing his unseen audience with an "I'm-right-here-with-you-good-folks" glance.

I don't recall all the details of what Governor Faubus said that night. But his words electrified Little Rock. By morning they shocked the United States. By noon the next day his message horrified the world.

Faubus' alleged reason for calling out the troops was that he had received information that caravans of automobiles filled with white supremacists were heading toward Little Rock from all over the state. He therefore declared Central High School off limits to Negroes. For some inexplicable reason he added that Horace Mann, a Negro high school, would be off limits to whites.

Then, from the chair of the highest office of the State of Arkansas, Governor Orval Eugene Faubus delivered the infamous words, "blood will run in the streets" if Negro pupils should attempt to enter Central High School.

In a half dozen ill-chosen words, Faubus made his contribution to the mass hysteria that was to grip the city of Little Rock for several months.

The citizens of Little Rock gathered on September 3 to gaze upon the incredible spectacle of an empty school building surrounded by 250 National Guard troops. At about eight fifteen in the morning, Central students started passing through the line of national guardsmen—all but the nine Negro students.

I had been in touch with their parents throughout the day. They were confused, and they were frightened. As the parents voiced their fears, they kept repeating Governor Faubus' words that "blood would run in the streets of Little Rock" should their teen-age children try to attend Central—the school to which they had been assigned by the school board.

Typical of the parents was Mrs. Birdie Eckford. "Mrs. Bates," she asked, "what do you think we should do? I am frightened. Not for myself but for the children. When I was a little girl, my mother and I saw a lynch mob dragging the body of a Negro man through the streets of Little Rock. We were told to get off the streets. We ran. And by cutting through side streets and alleys, we managed to make it to the home of a friend. But we were close enough to hear the screams of the mob, close enough to smell the sickening odor of burning flesh. And, Mrs. Bates, they took the pews from Bethel Church to make the fire. They burned the body of this Negro man right at the edge of the Negro business section.

"Mrs. Bates, do you think this will happen again?"

I reminded Mrs. Eckford that Little Rock was a different city now. Different from 1927, when the lynching and the burning had taken place. True, Governor Faubus spoke of blood. But in the next breath he had said that he called out the guardsmen to protect life and property against violence. Surely he meant the lives of the Negro students as well as white! No, it was inconceivable that troops, and responsible citizens, would stand by and let a mob attack children.

62

The NAACP attorneys, Wiley Branton and Thurgood Marshall, appealed to Federal Judge Ronald N. Davies for instruction. Their question was, in effect: What do we do now? The judge stated that "he was accepting the Governor's statement at face value—that his purpose in calling out the Guard was to protect 'life and property' against possible mob violence." Therefore, Judge Davies directed the school board again to put its plan for integration into operation immediately.

On the afternoon of the same day, September 3, when the school was scheduled to open, Superintendent Blossom called a meeting of leading Negro citizens and the parents of the nine children. I was not notified of the meeting, but the parents called me and asked me to be present. At the meeting Superintendent Blossom instructed the parents *not* to accompany their children the next morning when they were scheduled to enter Central. "If violence breaks out," the Superintendent told them, "it will be easier to protect the children if the adults aren't there."

During the conference Superintendent Blossom had given us little assurance that the children would be adequately protected. As we left the building, I was aware of how deeply worried the parents were, although they did not voice their fears.

About ten o'clock that night I was alone in the downstairs recreation room, my mind still occupied by the problems raised during the conference. L. C. appeared in the doorway. With him was a local reporter whom I had known for some time.

Words began pouring from the young reporter. "Look, Daisy," he said anxiously. "I know about the Superintendent's instructions. I know he said the children must go alone to Central in the morning. But let me tell you, this is murder! I heard those people today. I've never seen anything like it. People I've known all my life—they've gone mad. They're totally without reason. You must know you can't expect much protection—if any—from the city police. Besides, the city police are barred from the school grounds!"

My friend's voice took on a pleading quality, as if there were something I could do. "I swear there must have been about five hundred people at the school today," he continued. "And new recruits are pouring into the city from outlying areas. Even from other states. By morning there could be several thousand."

"What do you think we should do?" I asked him.

"I really don't know," he answered. "I really don't know."

The young reporter left. I sat huddled in my chair, dazed, trying to think, yet not knowing what to do. I don't recall how much time went by—a few minutes, an hour, or more—before some neighbors entered. One of them was the Reverend J. C. Crenchaw, President of the Little Rock branch of the NAACP.

His presence in my house immediately gave me an idea.

"Maybe," I said, "maybe we could round up a few ministers to go with the children tomorrow. Maybe then the mob wouldn't attack them. Maybe with the ministers by their side—"

Mr. Crenchaw caught on to the idea right away. "We can try, Daisy. At least we can try. Maybe this is the answer."

I called a white minister, Rev. Dunbar Ogden, Jr., President of the Interracial Ministerial Alliance. I did not know Mr. Ogden. I explained the situation, then asked if he thought

64

he could get some ministers to go with the children to school the next morning.

"Well, Mrs. Bates, I don't know," he said. "I'll call some of the ministers and see what they think about it. You know, this is a new idea to me."

I said the idea was new to me, too; and that it had just occurred to me moments before. Tensely I waited for his return call. When it came, he sounded apologetic. The white ministers he had talked to had questioned whether it was the thing to do. Some of the Negro ministers had pointed out that the Superintendent of Schools had asked that no Negro adults go with the children, and that in view of this they felt they shouldn't go. Then he added gently, "I'll keep trying— and, God willing, I'll be there."

Next I called the city police. I explained to the officer in charge that we were concerned about the safety of the children and that we were trying to get ministers to accompany them to school the next morning. I said that the children would assemble at eight thirty at Twelfth Street and Park Avenue. I asked whether a police car could be stationed there to protect the children until the ministers arrived.

The police officer promised to have a squad car there at eight o'clock. "But you realize," he warned, "that our men cannot go any closer than that to the school. The school is off limits to the city police while it's 'occupied' by the Arkansas National Guardsmen."

By now it was two thirty in the morning. Still, the parents had to be called about the change in plan. At three o'clock I completed my last call, explaining to the parents where the children were to assemble and the plan about the ministers. Suddenly I remembered Elizabeth Eckford. Her family had no telephone. Should I go to the Union Station and search for her father? Someone had once told me that he had a night job there. Tired in mind and body, I decided to handle the matter early in the morning. I stumbled into bed.

A few hours later, at about eight fifteen in the morning, L. C. and I started driving to Twelfth Street and Park Avenue. On the way I checked out in my mind the possibilities that awaited us. The ministers might be there—or again they might not. Mr. Ogden, failing to find anyone to accompany him, understandably might not arrive. Would the police be there? How many? And what if—

The bulletin over the car radio interrupted. The voice announced: "A Negro girl is being mobbed at Central High. . . ."

"Oh, my God!" I cried. "It must be Elizabeth! I forgot to notify her where to meet us!"

L. C. jumped out of the car and rushed to find her. I drove on to Twelfth Street. There were the ministers—two white— Mr. Ogden and Rev. Will Campbell, of the National Council of Churches, Nashville, Tennessee—and two colored—the Reverend Z. Z. Driver, of the African Methodist Episcopal Church, and the Reverend Harry Bass, of the Methodist Church. With them also was Mr. Ogden's twenty-one-year-old son, David. The children were already there. And, yes, the police had come as promised. All of the children were there— all except Elizabeth.

Soon L. C. rushed up with the news that Elizabeth finally was free of the mob. He had seen her on a bus as it pulled away.

The children set out, two ministers in front of them, two behind. They proceeded in that formation until they approached the beginning of the long line of guardsmen. At this point they had their first brush with the mob. They were jostled and shoved. As they made their way toward the school grounds, the ministers and their charges attempted to pass the guardsmen surrounding Central High. A National Guard captain stopped them. He told Mr. Ogden he could not allow them to pass through the guard line. When Mr. Ogden asked why, the captain said it was by order of Governor Faubus.

The ministers returned to the car with the students and Mr. Ogden reported what the captain of the guardsmen had said. I told him that in view of the school board's statement the previous evening that Central High School would be open to Negro students in the morning, it was my feeling that the students should go immediately to the office of the Superintendent for further instructions.

When we arrived at the office, the Superintendent was out. When he failed to return within an hour, I suggested that we appeal to the United States Attorney, Osro Cobb, since Federal Judge Davies had ordered the Federal Bureau of Investigation, under the direction of the United States Attorney, to conduct a thorough investigation into who was responsible for the interference with the Court's integration order.

Mr. Cobb looked surprised when we entered his office. I told him that we were there because the students had been denied admittance to Central High School by the national guardsmen and we wanted to know what action, if any, his office planned to take.

After questioning the pupils, he directed them to the office of the FBI, where they gave a detailed report of what had happened to them that morning.

I might add here that during the school year the FBI

interviewed hundreds of persons. Many of those who had participated in the mob could easily have been identified from photographs taken in front of the school. Yet no action was taken against anyone by the office of the United States Attorney, Osro Cobb, or the Department of Justice.

CHAPTER V

.

SHE WALKED ALONE

Dr. Benjamin Fine was then education editor of *The New York Times*. He had years before won for his newspaper a Pulitzer prize. He was among the first reporters on the scene to cover the Little Rock story.

A few days after the National Guard blocked the Negro children's entrance to the school, Ben showed up at my house. He paced the floor nervously, rubbing his hands together as he talked.

"Daisy, they spat in my face. They called me a 'dirty Jew.' I've been a marked man ever since the day Elizabeth tried to enter Central. I never told you what happened that day. I tried not to think about it. Maybe I was ashamed to admit to you or to myself that white men and women could be so beastly cruel.

"I was standing in front of the school that day. Suddenly there was a shout—'They're here! The niggers are coming!' I saw a sweet little girl who looked about fifteen, walking alone. She tried several times to pass through the guards. The last time she tried, they put their bayonets in front of her. When they did this, she became panicky. For a moment she just stood there trembling. Then she seemed to calm down and started walking toward the bus stop with the mob baying at her heels like a pack of hounds. The women were shouting, 'Get her! Lynch her!' The men were yelling, 'Go home, you bastard of a black bitch!' She finally made it to the bus stop and sat down on the bench. I sat down beside her and said, 'I'm a reporter from *The New York Times,* may I have your name?' She just sat there, her head down. Tears were streaming down her cheeks from under her sun glasses. Daisy, I don't know what made me put my arm around her, lifting her chin, saying, 'Don't let them see you cry.' Maybe she reminded me of my fifteen-year-old daughter, Jill.

"There must have been five hundred around us by this time. I vaguely remember someone hollering, 'Get a rope and drag her over to this tree.' Suddenly I saw a white-haired, kind-faced woman fighting her way through the mob. She looked at Elizabeth, and then screamed at the mob, 'Leave this child alone! Why are you tormenting her? Six months from now, you will hang your heads in shame.' The mob shouted, 'Another nigger-lover. Get out of here!' The woman, who I found out later was Mrs. Grace Lorch, the wife of Dr. Lee Lorch, professor at Philander Smith College, turned to me and said, 'We have to°do something. Let's try to get a cab.'

"We took Elizabeth across the street to the drugstore. I remained on the sidewalk with Elizabeth while Mrs. Lorch tried to enter the drugstore to call a cab. But the hoodlums slammed the door in her face and wouldn't let her in. She pleaded with them to call a cab for the child. They closed in on her saying, 'Get out of here, you bitch! Just then the city bus came. Mrs. Lorch and Elizabeth got on. Elizabeth must have been in a state of shock. She never uttered a word. When the bus pulled away, the mob closed in around me. 'We saw you put your arm around that little bitch. Now it's your turn.' A drab, middle-aged woman said viciously, 'Grab him and kick him in the balls!' A girl I had seen hustling in one of the local bars screamed, 'A dirty New York Jew! Get him!' A man asked me, 'Are you a Jew?' I said, 'Yes.' He then said to the mob, 'Let him be! We'll take care of him later.'

"The irony of it all, Daisy, is that during all this time the national guardsmen made no effort to protect Elizabeth or to help me. Instead, they threatened to have me arrested—for inciting to riot."

Elizabeth, whose dignity and control in the face of jeering mobsters had been filmed by television cameras and recorded in pictures flashed to newspapers over the world, had overnight become a national heroine. During the next few days newspaper reporters besieged her home, wanting to talk to her. The first day that her parents agreed she might come out of seclusion, she came to my house where the reporters awaited her. Elizabeth was very quiet, speaking only when

71

spoken to. I took her to my bedroom to talk before I let the reporters see her. I asked how she felt now. Suddenly all her pent-up emotion flared.

"Why am I here?" she said, turning blazing eyes on me. "Why are you so interested in my welfare now? You didn't care enough to notify me of the change of plans—"

I walked over and reached out to her. Before she turned her back on me, I saw tears gathering in her eyes. My heart was breaking for this young girl who stood there trying to stifle her sobs. How could I explain that frantic early morning when at three o'clock my mind had gone on strike?

In the ensuing weeks Elizabeth took part in all the activities of the nine—press conferences, attendance at court, studying with professors at nearby Philander Smith College. She was present, that is, but never really a part of things. The hurt had been too deep.

On the two nights she stayed at my home I was awakened by the screams in her sleep, as she relived in her dreams the terrifying mob scenes at Central. The only times Elizabeth showed real excitement were when Thurgood Marshall met the children and explained the meaning of what had happened in court. As he talked, she would listen raptly, a faint smile on her face. It was obvious he was her hero.

Little by little Elizabeth came out of her shell. Up to now she had never talked about what happened to her at Central. Once when we were alone in the downstairs recreation room of my house, I asked her simply, "Elizabeth, do you think you can talk about it now?"

She remained quiet for a long time. Then she began to speak.

"You remember the day before we were to go in, we met Superintendent Blossom at the school board office. He told us what the mob might say and do but he never told us we wouldn't have any protection. He told our parents not to come because he wouldn't be able to protect the children if they did.

"That night I was so excited I couldn't sleep. The next morning I was about the first one up. While I was pressing my black and white dress—I had made it to wear on the first day of school—my little brother turned on the TV set. They started telling about a large crowd gathered at the school. The man on TV said he wondered if we were going to show up that morning. Mother called from the kitchen, where she was fixing breakfast, 'Turn that TV off!' She was so upset and worried. I wanted to comfort her, so I said, 'Mother, don't worry.'

"Dad was walking back and forth, from room to room, with a sad expression. He was chewing on his pipe and he had a cigar in his hand, but he didn't light either one. It would have been funny, only he was so nervous.

"Before I left home Mother called us into the living-room. She said we should have a word of prayer. Then I caught the bus and got off a block from the school. I saw a large crowd of people standing across the street from the soldiers guarding Central. As I walked on, the crowd suddenly got very quiet. Superintendent Blossom had told us to enter by the front door. I looked at all the people and thought, 'Maybe I will be safer if I walk down the block to the front entrance behind the guards.'

"At the corner I tried to pass through the long line of guards around the school so as to enter the grounds behind them. One of the guards pointed across the street. So I pointed in the same direction and asked whether he meant for me to cross the street and walk down. He nodded 'yes.' So, I

73

walked across the street conscious of the crowd that stood there, but they moved away from me.

"For a moment all I could hear was the shuffling of their feet. Then someone shouted, 'Here she comes, get ready!' I moved away from the crowd on the sidewalk and into the street. If the mob came at me I could then cross back over so the guards could protect me.

"The crowd moved in closer and then began to follow me, calling me names. I still wasn't afraid. Just a little bit nervous. Then my knees started to shake all of a sudden and I wondered whether I could make it to the center entrance a block away. It was the longest block I ever walked in my whole life.

"Even so, I still wasn't too scared because all the time I kept thinking that the guards would protect me.

"When I got right in front of the school, I went up to a guard again. But this time he just looked straight ahead and didn't move to let me pass him. I didn't know what to do. Then I looked and saw that the path leading to the front entrance was a little further ahead. So I walked until I was right in front of the path to the front door.

"I stood looking at the school—it looked so big! Just then the guards let some white students go through.

"The crowd was quiet. I guess they were waiting to see what was going to happen. When I was able to steady my knees, I walked up to the guard who had let the white students in. He too didn't move. When I tried to squeeze past him, he raised his bayonet and then the other guards closed in and they raised their bayonets.

"They glared at me with a mean look and I was very frightened and didn't know what to do. I turned around and the crowd came toward me.

74

"They moved closer and closer. Somebody started yelling, 'Lynch her! Lynch her!'

"I tried to see a friendly face somewhere in the mob—someone who maybe would help. I looked into the face of an old woman and it seemed a kind face, but when I looked at her again, she spat on me.

"They came closer, shouting, 'No nigger bitch is going to get in our school. Get out of here!'

"I turned back to the guards but their faces told me I wouldn't get help from them. Then I looked down the block and saw a bench at the bus stop. I thought, 'If I can only get there I will be safe.' I don't know why the bench seemed a safe place to me, but I started walking toward it. I tried to close my mind to what they were shouting, and kept saying to myself, 'If I can only make it to the bench I will be safe.'

"When I finally got there, I don't think I could have gone another step. I sat down and the mob crowded up and began shouting all over again. Someone hollered, 'Drag her over to this tree! Let's take care of the nigger.' Just then a white man sat down beside me, put his arm around me and patted my shoulder. He raised my chin and said, 'Don't let them see you cry.'

"Then, a white lady—she was very nice—she came over to me on the bench. She spoke to me but I don't remember now what she said. She put me on the bus and sat next to me. She asked me my name and tried to talk to me but I don't think I answered. I can't remember much about the bus ride, but the next thing I remember I was standing in front of the School for the Blind, where Mother works.

"I thought, 'Maybe she isn't here. But she has to be here!' So I ran upstairs, and I think some teachers tried to talk to me, but I kept running until I reached Mother's classroom.

"Mother was standing at the window with her head bowed, but she must have sensed I was there because she turned around. She looked as if she had been crying, and I wanted to tell her I was all right. But I couldn't speak. She put her arms around me and I cried."

CHAPTER VI

OUT OF THE HILLS...

AFTER the attack on Elizabeth, hysteria in all of its madness enveloped the city. Racial feelings were at a fever pitch. Each day new recruits for the hate groups poured into the city from all parts of the State, and the effectiveness of the local police in dealing with these groups steadily diminished in direct ratio to the growth of the groups under the protective arm of the State-controlled National Guard.

Presently the local police were rendered almost totally impotent, and Mayor Woodrow Mann declared: "I am sure a great majority of the people in Little Rock share my deep resentment at the manner in which the Governor has chosen to use this city as a pawn in what clearly is a political design of his own."

Mayor Mann was not alone in interpreting Faubus' sensational act of calling out the National Guard as a political maneuver. Many political observers concurred, feeling that it was a desperate bid for a third term. By using the State's military power to defy Federal laws Governor Faubus, in effect, proclaimed that the rights of the State superseded the rights of the Federal government. The issue of State versus Federal rights, of course, is a favorite one with most Southerners and was the ostensible reason for the South's seceding from the Union during Abraham Lincoln's presidency. It brought Faubus immediate political dividends in the form of a widespread, fanatical following. Where for years he had been considered a rather colorless man, he was now a hero —indispensable to many who were not necessarily rabid segregationists.

Only one Arkansas governor had ever been successful in his bid for a third term; now there was little doubt, if any, that Faubus would be elected to a third if he decided to run.

At forty-seven Orval Faubus had traveled a long strange road from his early beginnings. He was born in the heart of the Ozark mountains, in Madison County, reputedly in a log cabin.

In 1936 he earnestly began running for office, seeking the nomination of State Representative in the Democratic primary and losing in a close vote. In 1938 he was elected Circuit Clerk and re-elected in 1940. In May, 1942, he enlisted in the Army and was sent to Officers' Candidate School and then served in Europe with the 320th Regiment of the Thirty-fifth

Infantry Division. When he was released from the Army in 1946, he had attained the rank of Major.

Immediately, he began running for public office again and lost in his bid for a county judgeship. However, Faubus was far from dead politically. In his first postwar campaign he had attracted the attention of big-time politicos who liked the way he spoke the language of the rural voters.

Now Faubus joined political forces with Sidney S. McMath, who was seeking his first term as Governor. Faubus proved invaluable. Not only did he campaign hard in a language the rural voters understood, but he also threw the full weight of the *Madison County Record,* a weekly newspaper he had bought shortly after his discharge from the Army, behind McMath's candidacy. So appreciative was McMath of Faubus' efforts that when elected Governor in 1948, he appointed Faubus a highway commissioner. Then, in 1951, Faubus became McMath's administrative assistant, and a year later was named State Highway Director, one of the most sought-after political jobs in Arkansas.

The McMath machine was made up largely of wealthy, sophisticated young men, who prided themselves on their "liberalism." They easily won the urban voters in Little Rock, as well as the industrialized areas of Fort Smith, Pine Bluff, Jonesboro, and the oil town of El Dorado. They were also victorious in other towns where labor and Negro votes were strong.

After serving two terms, McMath made a bid for a third in 1952. He was opposed by a gentle-faced, white-haired judge from eastern Arkansas, Francis A. Cherry, who had discarded his judicial robes, rolled up his sleeves, and hit the hot, dusty campaign trail.

Arkansas is predominantly a rural state. In 1950 only 33

per cent of its population was made up of urban dwellers. The decade 1940-1950 saw the exodus of many Negro share-croppers to northern cities. By the decade's end the white population of the state stood at 77 per cent, the Negro at 22 per cent.

Possibly more than in any other southern state, the Arkansan is dependent less on industry than on nature for his material well-being, as has been pointed out by the Arkansas historian, John Gould Fletcher.

The State is divided roughly into two regions—the Ozarks and the Ouachita Uplands—the whole forming a crescent of hill country, rich in beauty as well as in such natural resources as coal, bauxite, apple and melon yields, and even diamonds. Elsewhere there are magnificent plains and lowlands, with the rich alluvial plains of the Arkansas and Mississippi Delta regions producing cotton—the state's biggest crop. In the Arkansas Delta, plantations of from three thousand to five thousand acres are not uncommon.

In his campaign against McMath, Francis Cherry, the Jonesboro judge, set out to capture the backwoods vote. He campaigned extensively through mountain and plains country alike, from the plantation counties of the east to the scenic mountains of the west. He talked to farmers about crops and better schools, and, as every candidate had done for generations, promised better roads. Cherry introduced the radio talkathon, speaking for hours on end, answering voters' questions. Farmers who had no radios of their own gathered around the combination general store and filling station in the nearest settlement to hear the judge.

When Cherry entered the primary race, odds were two to one in favor of McMath. But as the talkathons continued,

Cherry won over more and more voters by his sincerity. He was elected Governor in 1952.

Governor Cherry had been in office little more than a year when the time arrived to carry on the tradition of working toward a second term. Filing date for the primaries closed on April 28, 1954. Minutes before the deadline, Orval Faubus quietly filed as candidate for Governor, joining Guy Jones and Gus McMillian along with the incumbent Cherry. Faubus had strong backing. Knowledgeable politicos liked his chances.

For one thing, he would be as attractive as Cherry to the rural voters. His home county, Madison, was still one of the most sparsely settled in the State, and his home town, Huntsville, had a population of about a thousand. He could talk easily about crops and farm prices and everything else dear to the farmers' hearts.

For another thing, labor, Negroes, and liberals in the cities assumed he had liberal inclinations because of his association with the McMath machine. In fact, he was even a target for attack by the White Citizens Council of Arkansas.

In the primary Jones and McMillian were eliminated, leaving Cherry and Faubus to compete in a run-off election. The battle that ensued was a bitter one. Cherry's supporters hit upon the idea of exposing the fact that in 1935 Faubus had attended Commonwealth College at Mena, Arkansas, an allegedly Communist institution. The college had been the subject of a State legislative inquiry and was subsequently closed as a "public nuisance" by court order in 1941. In 1949 the institution was placed on the United States Attorney General's subversive list.

However, the unearthing and publicizing of Faubus' record as a student at the since largely forgotten and now defunct Commonwealth College backfired. Faubus and his supporters effectively turned the tables on their detractors. Faubus presented himself on television as being the victim of a below-the-belt tactic. Sure, he acknowledged, he did attend Commonwealth. But, he pleaded, he was then a young man, son of a poor farmer, a scholarship recipient who was innocently drawn to an institution whose character he knew nothing about. Obviously the voters were won over by this defense.

Another political factor that helped to swing the balance in Faubus' favor was the defeat of his friend and mentor, Sidney S. McMath, who had opposed John L. McClellan in the primary race for United States senator. With his defeat McMath threw his State political support over to Faubus.

In spite of the early unbelievable odds against his success, Faubus was elected Governor of Arkansas in 1954, for the first of five consecutive terms.

Faubus' administration was not without its political ironies. Faubus and McMath broke political ties. When the National Guard issue arose during the integration struggle, both men later hurled bitter charges at each other. During one exchange McMath was quoted in the newspapers as saying that the only mistake he (McMath) had made as Governor was "to build that one paved road in Madison County that let Faubus out."

I have often reflected on that remark. What would Little Rock be like today, I wonder, if indeed that road had not been built?

Thurgood Marshall and Wiley Branton, attorneys for the National Association for the Advancement of Colored People, appeared in the United States District Federal Court to ask for an injunction against interference with the integration of Central High School by the Governor and the Adjutant General of Arkansas and the Unit Commander of the National Guard. The hearing was set for Friday, September 20.

In the midst of the hearing, after being overruled several times by the bench, Governor Faubus' attorneys shocked the court and astounded Thurgood Marshall, the rugged civil rights attorney whose record for victories before the Supreme Court is second to none, by gathering up their stacks of briefs and petitions and announcing to the court that they were leaving.

Judge Ronald N. Davies, a short slender man with an oval face and dark hair, raised himself slightly in his chair and peered down at the attorneys with a puzzled expression, as though doubting his own ears. As Faubus' lawyers made what I'm sure they considered a dignified exit, Mr. Marshall turned to Wiley Branton. "Now," he sighed, "I've *really* seen everything!"

The courtroom buzzed with excitement. Judge Davies straightened his shoulders, pounded his gavel on the mahogany desk, and announced in his precise voice: "The hearing will continue." Later the judge granted the injunction barring the Governor's use of National Guard troops to interfere with integration at Central High School.

That evening Governor Faubus went on television and announced that he had withdrawn the national guardsmen in compliance with the Federal Court order. Having created the mob, he now tried to shift the responsibility onto the Negro community. He said he hoped the Negro pupils, of their own volition, would refrain from exercising their rights

83

under the court order by staying away from Central High until such time as school integration could be accomplished without violence. Shortly after his broadcast, the Governor departed for the Southern Governors' Conference at Sea Island, Georgia.

CHAPTER VII

A CITY GRIPPED
BY FEAR AND TERROR

LITTLE ROCK was tense and solemn the day of September twenty-second before the volcano of hate finally erupted in a mighty explosion heard around the world. Except for the urgent, erratic pealing of church bells, the streets were ominously quiet. Hidden behind locked doors were the city's children, who usually were outside at this time, laughing, roller skating, playing ball, and jumping rope. Few strollers took advantage of the pleasant sunny weather; if they had no urgent business outdoors they remained indoors with their children, occupying themselves with the minute details of their personal lives. To anyone familiar with Little Rock on a sunny Sunday afternoon, the city seemed to have stopped breathing.

Some of the clergy had called for a city-wide day of prayer for peace, and many earnest men and women, both black and white, silently appealed to God for help and guidance. But many others, including ministers of God, screamed for action against what they deemed an affront to the Southern way of life, to God and the white people. Before the day ended Mrs. Margaret Jackson, head of the Mothers League, issued a statement calling for an all-out demonstration in front of the school the next morning.

Elizabeth Eckford came by my home after church. "Mrs. Bates," she asked, "now that the National Guard's gone, what's going to happen? Are we going in tomorrow? Will we have protection this time?"

"I'm sure you will, dear," I told her.

I explained to her that Chief of Police Marvin Potts was mobilizing his police forces, that the school board was meeting, and that by the day's end we should know the extent of the protection that would be given.

"Did you know," asked Elizabeth, "two white ministers and a lawyer visited all of our homes Friday and prayed with us?"

"Yes." I smiled. "I knew." The ministers had come to the *State Press* office earlier Friday to tell me, "We came to pray with you." I had just finished reading an article concerning the Reverend Wesley Pruden, pastor of the Broadmoor Baptist Church and a leader in the Capital Citizens Council. I had been thinking about the hundreds of ministers who had not spoken out against the mobsters who had been terrorizing the city in the last seventeen days. I had heard that many ministers were privately pro-integration, and I wished that these men were even half as vocal as Mr. Pruden.

Therefore I may have been a bit impatient when I replied to my visitors: "I don't need prayer. If you are really interested in doing something to help, go visit the homes of the nine children—pray with them—they are the ones who will have to face the mob."

The ministers were the Reverend Bert Cartwright, of the Methodist Church, and the Reverend William Campbell of the National Council of Churches, the Nashville minister who had been among those accompanying the children the first day. With them was C. C. Mercer, a Negro attorney.

Superintendent of Schools Blossom called me late that night and asked me to notify the children to meet the next morning at my house where they were to await further instructions as to how to get them to school. Assistant Chief of Police Gene Smith, I was told, would be in charge of the city police at the school.

87

CHAPTER VIII

THE VOLCANO OF HATE ERUPTS

On Monday morning, September 23, all nine children, accompanied by their parents, arrived at my home before eight o'clock. All but two parents had to leave for work immediately. The two who remained were Oscar Eckford, a night worker, and Mrs. Imogene Brown, an unemployed practical nurse.

Reporters came and went. They wanted to know whether the children were going to school. A few of the newspapermen called me aside, lowered their voices, and asked, "Mrs. Bates, are you really sending the children to Central? The mob there is really vicious now."

There were several radio outlets in our home and the children stationed themselves all over the house to listen. Radio commentators were broadcasting sidewalk interviews with men and women in the mob gathered in front of Central. A man was saying, "Just let those niggers show up! Just let 'em try!" Someone else said, "We won't stand for our schools being integrated. If we let 'em in, next thing they'll be marrying our daughters."

None of us said anything, but all of us were watching the hands of the clock move closer to eight thirty. The radios blared, but the children were strangely silent. Elizabeth sat alone, almost motionless. Carlotta and Ernest walked restlessly from room to room. The faces of all were solemn but determined.

Once when I entered the living-room I saw Mrs. Brown seated on the sofa, her hands clasped tightly in her lap, her eyes closed, her lips moving in prayer. Across the room Mr. Eckford sat with bowed head. For the first time I found that I was praying, too.

At last the call came from the police. They told us it would be safer to take a roundabout route to the school. They would meet us near Central and escort the children through a side entrance.

The white newsmen left my home for Central High. The Negro reporters remained, seating themselves around the kitchen table drinking coffee. They were: L. Alex Wilson, general manager and editor of the *Tri-State Defender,* of Memphis, Tennessee; James Hicks, managing editor of the *New York Amsterdam News;* Moses J. Newsome of the *Afro-American,* of Baltimore, Maryland, and Earl Davy, *State Press* photographer.

I told them they must take a different route from the one the children would take, but that if they were at the Sixteenth

Street and Park Avenue entrance to Central, they would be able to see the nine enter the school.

We had two cars. I went in the first car with some of the children and C. C. Mercer. Frank Smith, field secretary of the NAACP, followed with the rest of the nine. To this day I cannot remember which of the nine were in our car. Nor can they.

As we approached the side entrance to the school, the main body of the mob was moving away from us. I got out of the car and told the children to go quickly. From the sidewalk I watched the police escort them through the door of the school. Someone in the mob saw them enter and yelled, "They're in! The niggers are in!"

The people on the fringes of the mob started moving toward us. A policeman rushed up to me. "Get back in the car, Mrs. Bates. Drive back the way you came, and fast!"

I tumbled into the car. Mr. Mercer was waiting at the wheel. The car radio was on and a hoarse-voiced announcer was saying: "The Negro children are being mobbed in front of the school." I knew the children were in the school and, for the moment, at least, safe. But who was being mobbed?

We sped back to the house to reassure Mrs. Brown and Mr. Eckford. Then I called the other parents at work to quiet their fears.

A series of false radio reports followed. Newscasters, broadcasting from the school grounds, reported that the children were being beaten and were running down the halls of the school, bloodstained; that the police were trying to get them out, but the nine children, hysterical with fright, had locked themselves in an empty classroom.

A young white lawyer, who was very close to Assistant Chief of Police Gene Smith, devised a plan by which he would keep me informed of the goings on inside the school. When I called him, he assured me that the reports were false. After each report I would check with him, then call the parents. Once Mr. Eckford screamed at me in exasperation, "Well, if it's not true why would they say such things on the air?"

"*The children have barricaded themselves inside the school, the mob is breaking through the barricades, and the police are powerless to rescue the children,*" we heard one breathless newscaster announce. Again I called and demanded to know what was going on. I was told that the children were safe, but the police didn't know how much longer their forces could control the mob, which had now grown to over a thousand.

Later that day we learned that a white teen-age girl had been slipping in and out of the school, issuing false reports to the radio broadcasters. They had put her statements on the air without checking them. Gene Smith, Assistant Chief of Police, had finally caught up with her and ordered her arrested.

One could say it was the answer to Mrs. Brown's prayer that the Negro reporters arrived at Central about five minutes ahead of us. Jimmy Hicks of the *Amsterdam News* later told me just what did happen that morning.

"We parked our car near the school and made a dash for the Sixteenth Street entrance. When the mob saw us, they yelled, 'Here they come!' and came rushing at us. The women screamed, 'Get the niggers! Get 'em!' About a thousand folk blocked the streets. One big burly guy swung at my head. I ducked. The blow landed on my shoulder, spinning me around. I ran between two parked cars which concealed me from the mob. Two men jumped on top of Earl Davy, dragging him into a bank of high grass. Others were kicking and beating him while the two held him. They took his press camera and threw it to the sidewalk and smashed it flat with their feet. Several men jumped on Alex Wilson, knocking him to the ground and kicking him in the stomach. As he was getting up, one of the mobsters hollered, 'Run, nigger!' Alex wouldn't run. The brute, with a brick in his hand, jumped on Alex's back, and raised the brick to crush Alex's skull.

" 'The niggers are in the school! The niggers are in the school!'

"The man jumped off Alex's back, calling to the others, 'Come on! The niggers are in!' The mobsters beating Davy, Newsome, and Wilson all charged toward the school like a pack of wild animals.

"We probably saved you and the children, but I know you saved us. Some of the mob had spotted me between the cars and were advancing on me with sticks and clubs. And when they charged toward the school, we got the hell out of there. But you know, during all that beating, Alex never let go of his hat."

The frenzied mob rushed the police barricades. One man was heard to say, "So they sneaked them in behind our back. That's all we need. Let's go get our shotguns!" Hysterical women helped to break the barricades and then urged the men to go in and "get the niggers out!" Some of the women screamed for their children to "Come out! Don't stay in there with those niggers!" About fifty students rushed out, crying, "They're in! They're in!"

Around eleven thirty, Gene Smith realized his police force was inadequate to hold the mob. He ordered the nine removed from the school. They were taken out through a delivery entrance in the rear of the school, placed in police cars and driven to their homes. When it was announced that the children had been removed, the reporters rushed to my home and asked me what was our next step. Would the nine return to Horace Mann, the all-Negro school? I said No, they were going to remain out of the school until the President of the United States guaranteed them protection within Central High School. This was interpreted by the reporters as my having requested troops.

The mob, thwarted in its attempt to put its hands on the Negro children, switched momentarily to another field of battle. They went after the "Yankee" reporters.

The entire *Life* magazine staff on the scene was beaten. Photographers Francis Miller and Gray Villet were slugged in the mouth. Writer Paul Welch was beaten in the face and cut on the neck. All three men were arrested for inciting a riot. After their release Mr. Miller said, in bitter sarcasm, that he was evidently arrested for striking a man's fist with his face.

Most of the citizens of Little Rock were stunned as they witnessed a savage rebirth of passion and racial hatred that had lain dormant since Reconstruction days. As dusk was falling, tension and fear grew. The mob spread throughout the city, venting its fury on any Negro in sight.

Two Negro women driving through the city were pulled from their car and beaten. Two Negro men in a truck were surrounded by the mob near the school and beaten, and their truck windows smashed with rocks. Mayor Woodrow Mann wired President Eisenhower for protection. The Justice Department called Harry Ashmore, editor of the *Arkansas Gazette,* and asked him to describe the situation. He said, "I'll give it to you in one sentence. The police have been routed, the mob is in the streets and we're close to a reign of terror."

That evening I sat in the semidarkened living-room with L. C. and reporters, watching the empty quiet street through our broken living-room window. The police car that had been assigned to guard our house was barely visible across the street. A cab stopped in front of the house. All of us stood up. I heard a soft click. L. C. had released the safety on his .45 automatic. Dr. G. P. Freeman, our next-door neighbor and dentist, was aimlessly running his hand along the barrel of a shotgun he held in his left hand. When Alex Wilson of the Memphis *Tri-State Defender* stepped from the cab, I breathed a sigh of relief. As he entered the house Alex said, "I had planned to return earlier, but the story of the mob was a little difficult to write." He took L. C.'s gun, saying, "I'll watch for a while." He took a seat in front of the window. I watched him place his light gray hat on the table near him. I thought, "What a guy! He took the brunt of the mob today, yet here he is, holding a gun to help protect *us*."

The radio commentator reported that teen-age mobs had taken to cars and were driving wildly through the streets throwing bottles and bricks into Negroes' homes and places of business. One of the white reporters jumped out of his seat. "Ye gods!" he demanded. "Aren't they *ever* going to stop? Such hate! I heard a woman say today, 'I hope they drag out nine dead niggers from that school.' "

I left the room to call the parents of the pupils to see whether they had adequate protection. They reported that the city police were on the job. About 10:30 P.M., I returned to the living-room. Brice Miller, reporter for the United Press International, was talking to L. C. I saw his photographer in the shadows across the street.

"What's up, Brice?" I asked.

"Oh, nothing. Just checking."

"Oh, come now," I said. "We've all heard the rumor that the mob would ride tonight, and this will probably be their first stop. Isn't that the reason your photographer is across the street?"

"Well, yes," he admitted.

"Where did you hear the rumor?"

"One of the segregationist students told me. She was so pleased to have a reporter hanging on her words. I, of course, notified the police and the FBI."

L. C. broke into the conversation. "Something's up—things are too quiet." He asked Brice Miller about the radio reports.

"Oh, they're just a bunch of wild kids getting in on the act. They're not the real dangerous ones," he guessed.

"Say, Freeman," said L. C., "maybe we should stand guard outside for a while."

L. C. got a shotgun from the closet and, with Dr. Freeman, went outside. I went into the kitchen to make coffee. Brice Miller followed. "Since I'm here," he said, "maybe you can give me the reaction of the parents to today's mob."

Just then L. C. rushed back into the house. "Something's up! A car just passed driving slow with its lights off and a bunch of tough-looking characters in it. And the police car outside is following it."

Miller plunged past L. C., calling his photographer. "Come on! This might be it." Not only his photographer but all the reporters except Alex Wilson followed him.

"Do you have plenty of ammunition for these guns?" Alex asked.

"Yes," L. C. said.

"Well, we'll be ready for them if they show up."

Dr. Freeman stood guard at the bedroom window, Alex Wilson at the living-room, and L. C. at the kitchen window. L. C. told me to turn out the lights and go downstairs. I turned out the lights and sat on the top step of the stairway. We heard the wail of sirens approaching us. The minutes seemed like hours as I sat in the darkened stairway waiting for something to happen.

"The police are back," said L. C. He opened the door and turned on the lights.

"Turn that light off!" commanded the policeman as he entered. "And stay away from the window." The policeman, a big, red-haired man, was tense with excitement. "We just stopped a motorcade of about one hundred cars, two blocks from here. When we followed that car that passed, we ran into the mob head on. We radioed for help and a whole group of city and Federal agents showed up. We found dynamite, guns, pistols, clubs, everything, in the cars. Some of the mob got away on foot, leaving their cars. We don't know what will happen tonight, so no one is to leave the house."

No one slept that night.

At about 2:30 A.M. the phone rang. I answered. A man's voice said, "We didn't get you last night, but we will. And you better not try to put those coons in our school!"

Just before dawn I went to the kitchen to make a fresh pot of coffee. L. C. was sitting by the window, his shotgun cradled in his arm. Dawn was breaking. I watched the sky turn from dull gray to pale pink as the sun's rays flashed across the horizon. The aroma of the coffee aroused Wilson and Freeman from their cramped sitting positions. They entered the kitchen looking tired and worn.

"And I thought I had it tough as a correspondent during the Second World War," said Alex.

"I'm going to stick to pulling teeth, myself," said Freeman.

CHAPTER IX

THE FEDERAL TROOPS MOVE IN

THE NEXT DAY the children remained at home. A tense and weary city waited to hear from the White House.

The reporters sat around our living-room, drinking coffee and arguing among themselves on what possible action the President might take.

That morning calls came into my home from NAACP people, from parents, business and professional people, all asking the same question. "Have you heard from the White House?"

Around 8:30 A.M. a city truck stopped in front of my house

and a tall, husky Negro man approached the door and rang the bell. "Mrs. Bates, have you heard anything from Washington?"

"No, not directly," I said, "but the President issued a proclamation . . . ."

Before I could explain what the proclamation said and what I hoped it meant, he exclaimed: "Proclamation be damned! We've had the Constitution since 1789 and I doubt whether those goons who took over our town yesterday can read. Last night they came into our neighborhood and rocked our homes, breaking windows, and all that. We've taken a lot because we didn't want to hurt the chances of Negro kids, but I doubt whether the Negroes are going to take much more without fighting back. I think I'll take the rest of the day off and check my shotgun and make sure it's in working condition." He walked away.

Just then another group of white reporters joined the others in my living-room.

"Why aren't you at Central?" I asked them.

"Ha! Are you kidding?" one of them replied, speaking for the rest. "There's a mob of about five hundred out there in front of the school—jeering the city police standing in front of the barricades. It's a mean-looking bunch, too. We got out of there when we saw the police arrest two of them for carrying taped rubber hoses filled with lead."

"Are there any reporters out there now?"

"A few, but they're sticking close together."

In midafternoon the city was electrified by the news that President Eisenhower had federalized all ten thousand men of the Arkansas National Guard units. He had also authorized Charles E. Wilson, Secretary of Defense, to send in such regular United States troops as he deemed necessary ". . . to enforce any order of the United States District Court for the Eastern District of Arkansas for the removal of obstruction of Justice in the State of Arkansas with respect to matters relating to enrollment and attendance at public schools in the Little Rock School District." Under the authorization of this order, the Secretary of Defense ordered 1,000 paratroopers to Little Rock from Fort Campbell, Kentucky. The soldiers were part of the 101st Airborne "Screaming Eagle" Division of the 327th Infantry Regiment.

When the Negro and white paratroopers arrived at Camp Robinson, an Army Base in the suburb of North Little Rock, there was a general exodus of newsmen from our house. One reporter called back to me, "Come on, Mrs. Bates, aren't you going to see the troops enter the city?"

"No," I replied, "but thank God they're here."

After the newsmen were gone, I walked out onto the lawn. I heard the deep drone of big planes, and it sounded like music to my ears. I walked around the yard. I saw other women standing in their yards, looking upward, listening. I heard the subdued laughter of children and realized how long it had been since I'd heard that sound. Kept within doors in recent days, they now spilled out onto yards and driveways. From an open kitchen doorway Mrs. Anderson was heard singing. "Nobody knows the trouble I've seen . . ." A fear-paralyzed city had begun to stir again.

Around 6 P.M., the long line of trucks, jeeps, and staff cars entered the heart of the city to the wailing sound of sirens and the dramatic flashing of lights from the police cars escorting the caravan to Central High School. The "Battle of Little Rock" was on.

Some of the citizens watching the arrival of the troops cried with relief. Others cursed the Federal Government for

100

"invading our city." One got the impression that the "Solid South" was no longer solid.

A young white reporter rushed to my house and grabbed me by the hands, swinging me around. "Daisy, they're here! The soldiers are here! Aren't you excited? Aren't you happy?"

"Excited, yes, but not happy," I said after getting myself unwhirled. "Any time it takes eleven thousand five hundred soldiers to assure nine Negro children their constitutional right in a democratic society, I can't be happy."

"I think I understand how you feel," the reporter said. "You're thinking about all the other southern Negro children who'll have to 'hit the line' someday."

"Yes, and I'm sure there will be many."

"What's the next move?" he asked. "Will the children be going back to Central tomorrow?"

I parried the question. I knew the parents would be on tenterhooks waiting to hear from me, and with the same question on their minds. I delayed calling them. I was awaiting a call from Superintendent Blossom. Finally, about 10 P.M., I called all the parents to tell them I had not heard from Mr. Blossom. I assumed that the mob would be at the school the next morning, and therefore decided that the children could not be sent to Central the next day, troops or not.

Shortly after midnight Mr. Blossom telephoned. "Mrs. Bates, I understand you instructed the children that they were not to go to Central in the morning."

"That is correct."

"But General Walker said that he is here to put the children in school. So you must have them at your house by eight thirty in the morning." Major General Edwin A. Walker, chief of the Arkansas Military District, had been put in command of the 101st Airborne Division and newly federalized Arkansas militia.

"I can't," I said. "I can't reach them. We have an agreement that if I want them, I will call *before* midnight. In order to get some sleep and avoid the harassing calls, they take their phones off the hook after midnight." How I wish I had done the same, I thought wearily, as I listened to the Superintendent's urgent tones. "I suppose I could go to each home, but I can't go alone," I said.

"I'll call Hawkins and Christophe and ask them to accompany you," Mr. Blossom said. "You may expect them shortly." Edwin Hawkins was Principal of Dunbar Junior High School and L. M. Christophe was Principal of Horace Mann High School, both Negro schools.

At about 1 A. M. the three of us set out. Our first stop was some eight blocks away, the home of fifteen-year-old Gloria Ray. We knocked for what seemed ten minutes before we got an answer. The door opened about three inches exposing the muzzle of a shotgun. Behind it stood Gloria's father.

"What do you want now?" was his none-too-cordial greeting, as he looked straight at me. He forgot—I hope that was the reason—to remove his finger from the trigger or at least to lower the gun.

My eyes were fixed on the muzzle, and I could sense that Hawkins and Christophe, standing behind me, were riveted in attention. In my most pleasant, friendliest voice, and trying to look at him instead of the gun, I said that the children were to be at my house by eight thirty the next morning, and that those were the instructions of Superintendent Blossom.

"I don't care if the President of the United States gave you those instructions!" he said irritably. "I won't let Gloria go. She's faced two mobs and that's enough."

Both Mr. Christophe and Mr. Hawkins assured him that with the Federal troops there, the children would be safe. We all, of course, added that the decision was up to him. At this point I asked if he wouldn't mind lowering his gun. He did. I told him if he changed his mind to bring Gloria to my house in the morning. Somewhat shakily we made our way to the car.

"Good Lord," sighed Mr. Christophe, "are we going to have to go through this with all nine sets of parents?"

The children's homes were widely scattered over Little Rock, and so our tour took better than three hours. Our encounter with Mr. Ray impressed on our minds the need to identify ourselves immediately upon entering the grounds of each home. But the cautious parents still greeted us with gun in hand, although they were a little more calm than Mr. Ray, and accepted the change in plans without objection.

At eight twenty-five the next morning, all the children except Gloria had arrived. My phone rang. "What time are we to be there, Mrs. Bates?" It was Gloria.

"They're all here now."

"Wait for me!" she said. "I'll be right over!"

In less than ten minutes, Mr. Ray, shy and smiling, led Gloria into the house. He looked down at his daughter with pride. "Here, Daisy, she's yours. She's determined to go. Take her. You seem to have more influence over her than I have, anyhow."

No sooner had Gloria joined the group then I was called to the telephone. A school official wanted to know whether the children were there. "All nine," I answered. I was told that a convoy for them was on its way.

While we waited, reporters were asking the nine how they felt, and the children, tense and excited, found it difficult to be articulate about the significance of the troops' mission. Half an hour crawled by. Jeff, standing at the window, called out, "The Army's here! They're here!"

Jeeps were rolling down Twenty-eighth Street. Two passed our house and parked at the end of the block, while two remained at the other end of the block. Paratroopers quickly jumped out and stood across the width of the street at each end of the block—those at the western end standing at attention facing west, and those at the eastern end facing east.

An Army station wagon stopped in front of our house. While photographers, perched precariously on the tops of cars and rooftops, went into action, the paratrooper in charge of the detail leaped out of the station wagon and started up our driveway. As he approached, I heard Minnijean say gleefully, "Oh, look at them, they're so—so soldierly! It gives you goose pimples to look at them!" And then she added solemnly, "For the first time in my life, I feel like an American citizen."

The officer was at the door, and as I opened it, he saluted and said, his voice ringing through the sudden quiet of the living-room where a number of friends and parents of the nine had gathered to witness this moment in history: "Mrs. Bates, we're ready for the children. We will return them to your home at three thirty o'clock."

I watched them follow him down the sidewalk. Another paratrooper held open the door of the station wagon, and they got in. Turning back into the room, my eyes none too dry, I saw the parents with tears of happiness in their eyes as they watched the group drive off.

Tense and dramatic events were taking place in and around the school while the Negro pupils were being transported by the troops of the 101st Airborne from my home to Central High.

Major General Edwin A. Walker, operation commander, was explaining to the student body, in the school auditorium, the duties and responsibilities of his troops.

"... You have nothing to fear from my soldiers and no one will interfere with your coming, going, or your peaceful pursuit of your studies. However, I would be less than honest if I failed to tell you that I intend to use all means necessary to prevent any interference with the execution of your school board's plan ..."

A block from the school, a small group of hard-core segregationists ignored Major James Meyers' orders to disperse peacefully and return to their homes. The major repeated the command when the surly, angry crowd refused to disperse. He was forced to radio for additional help. About thirty soldiers answered the emergency call "on the double," wearing steel helmets, carrying bayonet fixed rifles, their gas masks in readiness, and "walkie-talkies" slung over their shoulders.

The soldiers lowered their rifles and moved slowly and deliberately into the crowd. The mob quickly gave way, shouting insults at the troops in the process. In a matter of minutes the streets, which for days had been littered with hate-filled mobs, cigarette butts, half-eaten sandwiches, and used flash bulbs, were strangely quiet.

At 9:22 A.M. the nine Negro pupils marched solemnly through the doors of Central High School, surrounded by twenty-two [Airborne troops] soldiers. An Army helicopter circled overhead. Around the massive brick schoolhouse 350 paratroopers stood grimly at attention. Scores of reporters, photographers, and TV cameramen made a mad dash for telephones, typewriters, and TV studios, and within minutes a world that had been holding its breath learned that the nine pupils, protected by the might of the United States military, had finally entered the "never-never land."

When classes ended that afternoon, the troops escorted the pupils to my home. Here we held the first of many conferences that were to take place during the hectic months ahead.

I looked into the face of each child, from the frail, ninety-pound Thelma Mothershed with a cardiac condition, to the well-built, sturdy Ernest Green, oldest of them all. They sat around the room, subdued and reflective—and understandably so. Too much had happened to them in these frenzied weeks to be otherwise.

I asked if they had a rough day. Not especially, they said. Some of the white pupils were friendly and had even invited them to lunch. Some were indifferent, and only a few showed open hostility.

Minnijean Brown reported that she had been invited by her classmates to join the glee club.

"Then why the long faces?" I wanted to know.

"Well," Ernest spoke up, "you don't expect us to be jumping for joy, do you?"

Someone said, "But Ernest, we *are* in Central, and that shouldn't make us feel sad exactly."

"Sure we're in Central," Ernest shot back, somewhat impatiently. "But how did we get in? We got in, finally, because we were protected by paratroops. Some victory!" he said sarcastically.

"Are you sorry," someone asked him, "that the President sent the troops?"

"No," said Ernest. "I'm only sorry it had to be that way."

CHAPTER X

ARREST

THE CITY COUNCIL met on October 31, at the city hall and ordered the wholesale arrest of NAACP officials. Specifically, the Council directed Little Rock Chief of Police Gene Smith "to arrest Daisy Bates, Reverend J. C. Crenchaw, and all other NAACP officials he could find."

The next day Mr. Crenchaw, who was President of the Little Rock NAACP branch, and I voluntarily surrendered ourselves to the police and were subsequently released on bond.

Also arrested were Mrs. Birdie Williams, President of the

North Little Rock NAACP branch, and W. A. Fair, a Vice-President of the branch.

All of us were charged with violating a city ordinance enacted two weeks before, requiring any organization, on request by any elected official of the city, to supply information regarding its membership, donors, amount of contributions, and expenditures. The information would become a matter of public record when it was filed with the City Clerk's office. The ordinance carried a penalty on conviction from $50 to $250 for each day's violation.

The arrests were widely publicized in the nation's press. The *New York Amsterdam News* had this to say at the time:

> The pictures showing white mobsters at Little Rock defying the Federal law on integration and beating and kicking Negro newsmen and their friends are plain as day.
>
> They show the faces of the mob leaders and they show the actual violence of the mob. In other words the pictures themselves make up a clear legal case by which the members of the mob could be put in jail.
>
> But here, almost a month after the violence of the mob at Little Rock, the authorities in that strange city have come forward with a new law by which they hope to jail, not the mobsters who defied the Federal Government in violence, but the NAACP leaders who were attempting to see that the law of the land was upheld.
>
> What kind of business is this? What manner of men are these who seek to jail those who have been wronged and make heroes of those who committed the wrongs?
>
> Frankly we have just about lost all patience with Little Rock. There was a time when we felt that Arkansas' crackpot governor was to blame for all the evils of Little Rock.
>
> But now we are not so sure. Mayor Woodrow Wilson Mann, who showed a reasonable degree of sanity when Faubus called out troops to block integration, is the man

who issued an order to the NAACP to make its records public and now we have the assistant mayor and the City Council demanding that Mrs. Daisy Bates and all NAACP officers of the city be arrested.

This is the most ridiculous thing we have heard of in a long, long time. It's sheer nonsense.

Here we have people who have trampled the Federal Constitution into the dust walking the streets free, and the city calling for the arrest of the very pillars of freedom in the city.

Have the people of Little Rock lost their minds? Or are they trying to kid the rest of the nation?

Everyone knows that as soon as the legal machinery of the NAACP gets this latest development into court any sane judge will dismiss it for what it is—another move to find a legal way to commit an illegal act.

There simply is no legal way to commit an illegal act and it's time that the people of the South be made to realize it.

The sane, decent-minded people of this nation would be much more sympathetic to the people of Little Rock if they were to spend their time tracking down and jailing the leaders of the recent mob violence there and creating a climate under which nine little children could peacefully attend school and get on with their education.

The trial of the NAACP leaders got under way on December 3 at 9:30 A.M. at Municipal Court. Judge Harry C. Robinson presided. Assistant City Attorney Joseph Brooks read the affidavit requesting the identity of the NAACP members and contributors. However, the City Attorney was unable to show to the court that Mr. Crenchaw had received a request to produce the Little Rock branch records. Mr. Brooks said it was undetermined from files in the Mayor's office whether Mr. Crenchaw had received a letter from the City. Charges against Mr. Crenchaw were thereby dropped.

The NAACP lawyers were Robert Carter, General Counsel for the association; Frank Reeves of Washington, D.C.;

George Howard of Pine Bluff, Arkansas, and J. R. Booker of Little Rock. They asked for a dismissal of the entire case on the grounds that I was not the President of the Little Rock branch and that I would not therefore have the records requested in my possession.

Judge Robinson then ruled, "I'm going to take judicial notice of the fact that if she is not head of the NAACP, she heads some branch or something in NAACP. I am going to hold that the ordinance is valid." He imposed a fine of $100, plus costs. The NAACP lawyers moved for an immediate appeal in the Circuit Court.

Pending a verdict on the appeal, the Court agreed to hold in abeyance the charges filed against the other NAACP officers, and would not invoke the penalties on the daily violations.

After failing to get a reversal in the Circuit Court and in the State Supreme Court, the attorneys appealed to the United States Supreme Court. Here the initial ruling was reversed.

As President of the NAACP State Conference of Branches, and as the publicized leader of the integration movement in Arkansas, I was singled out for "special treatment."

Two flaming crosses were burned on our property. The first, a six-foot gasoline-soaked structure, was stuck into our front lawn just after dusk. At the base of the cross was scrawled: "GO BACK TO AFRICA! KKK." The second cross was placed against the front of our house, lit, and the flames began to catch. Fortunately the fire was discovered by a neighbor, and we extinguished it before any serious damage had been done.

A rock was thrown through our living-room window and it barely missed me. A few nights later, a volley of shots was fired at our house from a passing car. One bullet pierced the window, entered the living-room and lodged in the wall. Other bullets ricocheted off the brick front of the house. We experienced the horrifying feeling that in our own home town there lived people who wanted us dead.

The violence intensified after Governor Faubus ordered out the national guardsmen. Often we were forced to call the police two and three times a day. We appealed to the Chief of Police for protection but he said that there was not enough manpower to station a policeman in our neighborhood. Our friends—concerned for our safety—organized a volunteer guard committee. We also installed floodlights along the wide eaves on the front of the house. The floodlights went on automatically when darkness came. Each evening our friends joined L. C. in the darkened carport and watched as cars cruised by filled with teen-agers shouting insults and exploding firecrackers in the street. Other cars filled with rough-looking, silent men drove slowly by.

It took many weeks for me to become accustomed to seeing revolvers lying on tables in my own home. And shotguns, loaded with buckshot, standing ready near the doors. As Ted Poston, covering the Little Rock story for the *New York Post,* remarked, the house, by necessity, had become a fortress.

After Governor Faubus declared himself on the side of those who sought to defy the law, the segregationists gained new status in the community. One of our leading daily newspapers, *The Arkansas Gazette,* criticized the Governor's action in an editorial on September 4, 1957, in these words:

> ... limited integration in the Little Rock schools was a local problem which had been well and wisely handled by respon-

sible local officials who have had and we believe still have the support of the majority of the people of the city! ... on Monday night he [Gov. Faubus] called out the National Guard and made it a national problem. It is one he must live with and the rest of us must suffer under.

After this editorial appeared, the *Gazette* became the object of an organized boycott by the segregationists; and its executive editor, Harry Ashmore, became a prime target of the vociferous minority's wrath. However, the majority of Little Rock citizens, frustrated by fear and violence, was unwilling to check what was happening. By default, an arrogant and persistent minority was left unopposed to engage in a reign of terror.

CHAPTER XI

THE EMBATTLED NINE

THE first few days at Central High School didn't add up to the most pleasant experience ever enjoyed by the nine Negro pupils, but neither was it the worst. In fact there were encouraging signs that the "Battle of Little Rock" was about to fade into history and that the process of integration might henceforth proceed without incident.

Minnijean was invited to join the school glee club, others were invited to lunch with their white fellow-students. A few days before the embattled nine entered the high school, the student newspaper, the *Tiger*, carried the following article, written by Jane Emery, co-editor of the paper:

> You are being watched! Today the world is watching you, the students of Central High. They want to know what your reactions, behavior, and impulses will be concerning a matter now before us. After all, as we see it, it settles down now to a matter of interpretation of law and order.
>
> Will you be stubborn, obstinate, or refuse to listen to both sides of the question? Will your knowledge of science help you determine your action or will you let customs, superstition, or tradition determine the decision for you?
>
> This is the chance that the youth of America has been waiting for. Through an open mind, broad outlook, wise thinking, and a careful choice you can prove that America's youth has not 'gone to the dogs,' that their moral, spiritual, and educational standards are not being lowered. This is the opportunity for you as citizens of Arkansas and students of Little Rock Central High to show the world that Arkansas is a progressive, thriving state of wide-awake alert people. It is a state which is rapidly growing and improving its social, health, and educational facilities. That it is a state with friendly, happy, and conscientious citizens who love and cherish their freedom.
>
> It has been said that life is just a chain of problems. If this is true, then this experience in making up your own mind and determining right from wrong will be of great value to you in life.
>
> The challenge is yours, as future adults of America, to prove your maturity, intelligence, and ability to make decisions by how you react, behave, and conduct yourself in this controversial question. What is your answer to this challenge?

It seemed altogether likely that the article in the *Tiger* had set the mood for the first few days of the Negro children's stay at Central. The mood was one of calm and acceptance.

Inside the school, classes returned to normal, and the business of educating students was resumed in earnest.

Outside the school, the situation was different. Newspapers soon were carrying the following story regarding the invitation extended to Minnijean to join the school's chorus:

> The League of Central High Mothers, an organization of white women opposing integration at Central High School, were up in arms last week over what they claimed was the selection of a Negro student to sing on the school's talent program.
>
> Mrs. Margaret C. Jackson, league president, said several white students reported that Minnijean Brown had been selected to sing "Tammy" on the program. Members of the league immediately phoned the school to protest, saying:
>
> "They [the Negro students] are not supposed to take part in things like that and we are simply protesting to the school people."

If soon thereafter the condition within the high school began to change from calm to turbulent, it merely reflected what was happening, or not happening, in the community itself.

What was happening was that the die-hard segregationists were not content to allow the issue to rest, come what may. They continued to display their passions of hate, much as prostitutes might peddle their own brand of passion. And apparently there is profit of a kind in the type of merchandising carried on by both these professions.

What was *not* happening in the city of Little Rock was equally shameful. The dramatic arrival of the 101st Airborne troops and the subsequent dissolution of the street mobs should have awakened "substantial" citizens to the realization that they were in part responsible for the chaos that had enveloped the city some weeks before. Now, in this period of calm, one hoped that they would provide constructive leadership. But by and large, the forthright militant action that the citizens were expecting of the elected officials, the prominent businessmen, and the religious leaders was, unfortunately, not forthcoming.

Evidently the citizens remembered all too well the action of their own City Councilmen. Eight out of ten of the Councilmen had signed a statement praising Governor Faubus for calling out the troops. Their statement said in part:

> ... We believe Governor Faubus took the proper course in calling out the Arkansas National Guard in this crisis to protect the lives and property of all our people.
>
> We commend him for his prompt action and sincerely hope that we will be permitted to work out our own problems within due process of law and without outside interference.
>
> We know that this is the desire of the overwhelming majority of the citizens of Little Rock.

The constant agitation of the segregationists, plus the inert leadership in the Little Rock community, had their effects inside Central High School. The relative calm and acceptance of the early weeks now gave way to repeated cruelties inflicted upon the nine Negro pupils. And once the harassments were allowed to begin, they continued with staggering regularity throughout the entire school year. The Negro pupils became constant targets for torture, both the physical and the psychological variety.

Minnijean Brown

Minnijean Brown, sixteen years old and in the eleventh grade, was tall, attractive, and outgoing. Her manner was friendly and good-natured. She sang well, was good at sports, and liked dancing. She was the oldest of four children and lived with her parents, Mr. and Mrs. W. B. Brown. Minnijean's feelings were quickly mirrored in her face. At school she was subjected to no greater pressure than were the other Negro pupils. However, the incidents in which she was involved were certainly more dramatic, if not spectacular.

The first of these incidents took place on October 2, 1957. Minnijean and Melba Pattillo were roughed up by several unidentified boys and girls in the corridors as they left their second class for the day. One girl deliberately ran into Minnijean, and a group of boys formed a line to block her entrance to her classroom. Then followed an incredible catalogue of violence:

Minnijean was kicked by a boy as she was going to her seat at "pep" assembly, prior to a football game.

She was threatened by a pupil who said, "I will chase you down the hall and kick all your teeth out the next time you do what you did yesterday afternoon." The boy alleged that she had made insulting gestures at him. Minnijean insisted she did not remember ever seeing him before. The boy was taken to the principal's office and reprimanded.

By the middle of December Minnijean had had enough. After repeated provocation by white pupils blocking her path as she attempted to reach a table in the cafeteria, she warned her persecutors that they might get something on their heads. On December 17, when chairs had been shoved in her way, she emptied her tray on the heads of two boys. These boys excused her, saying that she had been annoyed so frequently they "didn't blame her for getting mad." The boys were sent home to change their clothing. But Minnijean was suspended for six days because of the incident.

Soon after she returned to her classes, a pupil emptied a bowl of hot soup on Minnijean. The reason he gave was that he remembered she had earlier spilled chili on two white boys. He was suspended for three days.

(This pupil was finally expelled on February 10, 1958, after showing his contempt for a teacher by ostentatiously spitting on the floor as he was leaving her classroom. He then went to the office of the Vice-Principal, Mrs. Elizabeth Huckaby, and called her a "bitch." The pupil's school record was filled with violations of school rules. He had been suspended approximately twenty-eight days since school opened the previous September.

When I was told that the school board had finally decided to expel him, I said, "With his record they either had to expel him or make him Principal.")

One of the many unprovoked attacks was witnessed by Mrs. Brown. Toward the end of January, she was waiting for Minnijean at the Fourteenth Street exit. At about 3:30 P.M., Minnijean came out of school and saw that her mother was parked at the curb. Minnijean quickened her steps as she made her way to the car. Just before she reached her mother, a pupil, Richard Boehler, came up in back of Minnijean and gave her a vicious kick. Mrs. Brown, seeing this cruel attack on her daughter, screamed and jumped from the car. She started toward the boy but a teacher, who had also seen the incident, apprehended the boy and took him to the office of the Vice-Principal for boys. Boehler, who had been suspended from school earlier that same day, stated that he kicked Minnijean because he "was dared to." He also claimed that Minnijean had stamped on his leg in French class, but he couldn't remember the day. During the subsequent investigation, one of the soldiers reported that Boehler had previously threatened Minnijean with a knife.

Mrs. Brown attempted to file charges against Boehler, but the prosecuting attorney, J. Frank Holt, refused to issue a warrant for his arrest. He said that it was a matter for the school authorities. The school officials, in turn, did not take any action because of Boehler's suspension earlier that day. Poor Minnijean remained at home for a few days until she could sit without pain.

On February 6 Minnijean was suspended for the second time. She walked into my house that afternoon. "They did it to me again," she began. "I just lost my temper. I know it will make it harder for the other kids, but I just couldn't take it any longer."

Pacing the floor, she told me how a girl had been pestering her for days. "When I entered the building this morning," she related, "this girl followed me from the first floor to the third floor, kicking me on the back of my legs and calling me names. As we were entering our homeroom, she called out, 'black bitch.'

"I turned and screamed, 'White trash! Why don't you leave me alone? If you weren't white trash, you wouldn't bother me!' " The girl looked startled for a moment. I started for my seat. She threw her pocketbook at me and hit me on the head with it. I picked up the bag. My first impulse was to knock the devil out of her with it."

"I'm glad you were able to restrain yourself," I said.

"Yes, I am, too," she acknowledged. "I threw the bag on the floor in front of her and walked away in disgust. Then, while I was eating my lunch in the cafeteria, during first lunch period, a character walked over to the table and deliberately dumped a hot bowl of soup on me. A national guardsman came over and took us to Mr. Powell's office. He told the Vice-Principal he had dumped the soup on me because he remembered I had poured chili on some white boys."

The other Negro students later told me they had reported this same student several times to school authorities for harassing them.

The Principal, Jess W. Mathews, suspended both Minnijean and the boy. The suspension notice he sent to her parents stated:

> Reinstated on probation January 13, 1958, with the agreement that she would not retaliate, verbally or physically, to any harassment but would leave the matter to the school authorities to handle.
>
> After provocation of girl student, she called the girl "white trash" after which the girl threw her purse at Minnijean.

Upon recommendation of Superintendent of Schools Virgil Blossom, the Board of Education expelled Minnijean for the remainder of the school term.

After Minnijean's expulsion the small group of students who began tormenting the Negro children began wearing printed cards that read: "One down and eight to go."

Robert Carter, NAACP attorney from New York, was in the city the day the school board announced Minnijean's expulsion.

"What can we do about Minnijean?" I asked him. "We can't let her remain out of school for four months."

After much discussion we decided to call Dr. Kenneth B. Clark, Professor of Psychology at the College of the City of New York. He and his wife, Dr. Mamie Clark, are directors of the Northside Center for Child Development, which is located in the same building as the New Lincoln High School in New York City. We asked Dr. Clark if it would be possible for Minnijean to enroll at New Lincoln for the spring term.

Dr. Clark said he would check with Dr. John Brooks, Principal of New Lincoln at that time, and would call me back. The return call came in less than an hour. Dr. Brooks had told him that the school would be delighted to have Minnijean as a student. The Board of Directors at New Lincoln subsequently granted her a scholarship.

When Minnijean arrived in New York she was warmly welcomed at the airport by the Clark family and several NAACP officials. A *New York Post* editorial, on February 19, 1958, had this to say:

> Our Town has long been a haven for refugees from all over the world. Their number will now be increased by one Negro American from Little Rock. Like all the others, Minnie Jean Brown, expelled from Central High School, will be looking for equality of opportunity. She will complete her year's education as a scholarship pupil at the New Lincoln School on W. 110th Street.
>
> Minnie's expulsion for "talking back" to a white girl who cursed and struck her (and was not penalized) climaxed a cruel ordeal. Superintendent of Schools Virgil Blossom, who supported enforcement of the desegregation decision, recommended exiling this girl. Thus the pernicious influence of Gov. Faubus continues to corrupt or intimidate men of better instinct.
>
> The grim truth seems to be that the white supremacists of Little Rock are gaining ground. Harassment of the few Negro students in Central High is increasing rather than abating. Although the school authorities have taken action against a few of the white offenders, integrationists and those who merely wish to obey the law are plainly on the defensive.
>
> When a Negro girl is so drastically penalized for reacting as a human being under fire, it is no wonder that white youngsters in the school feel safe to resume the business of bullying. The school board, in expelling Minnie Jean, has

put its stamp of approval on the segregationalist strategy of terror.

Minnie Jean will find the demarcation line here less obvious. But part of the education she gets in Our Town will be the knowledge that we too practice racial discrimination, though more subtly than the folks back home. We hope it doesn't come as too much of a shock to her to discover that the difference between New York and Little Rock is not as great as it should be. Possibly her arrival will inspire us to be worthy of her, and of the cause for which she and other Southern Negro children have stood so stoically and so valiantly. Little Rock's loss is our proud acquisition.

While attending New Lincoln School, Minnijean lived with the Clarks, was mothered by Mamie, was in constant friendly combat with the Clarks' fourteen-year-old son, Hilton, and learned how to study with their teen-age daughter, Kate.

Minnijean graduated from New Lincoln on June 5, 1959.

Jefferson Thomas

Young fifteen-year-old Jefferson Thomas was a slim, quiet, soft-spoken boy. At the age of ten he dreamed of becoming a great architect. As he grew older he realized that his dream would probably never become a reality because, being a Negro, he was denied the right to attend the schools that offered the basic preparatory courses. Yet he was prepared to fight for his dream.

> I dream a world where man
> No other man will scorn,
> Where love will bless the earth
> And peace its paths adorn.
> I dream a world where all
> Will know sweet freedom's way,

Where greed no longer saps the soul
Nor avarice blights our day.
A world I dream where black or white,
Whatever race you be,
Will share the bounties of the earth
And every man is free,
Where wretchedness will hang its head
And joy, like a pearl,
Attends the needs of all mankind—
Of such I dream, my world!

—from "Troubled Island"
by Langston Hughes

After school each day I kept careful notes on the physical violence and psychological warfare directed against the nine students. And each day I wondered where they got the courage to re-enter the dimly lit corridors of Central High School to face new provocations and new assaults on their bodies as well as their dignity.

Next to Minnijean, Jefferson was the one singled out for the segregationists' wrath. Jefferson, son of Mr. and Mrs. Ellis Thomas, was the youngest of seven children. He knew when he entered Central that he, as well as the other Negro students, would have to give up all extracurricular activities he had enjoyed at his previous school. No longer would he be able to hear the cheers of his fellow students as he streaked across the finish line during a track meet. At Dunbar Junior High School he was an outstanding track star, a school hero who had won several awards for athletic prowess. At Dunbar, he was also President of the Student Council. He was now well aware that at Central he simply could not "belong." This was made crystal clear to the nine Negro pupils by the school authorities at the time the children were being selected from approximately eighty applicants who requested to be

123

transferred to Central. Some of the pupils who applied, who played on the football team or were music majors, withdrew their applications after being informed that they could not play in the school band or participate in sports.

The school board, under the School Assignment Law, which gave it the authority to place students in any school in the district, assigned the nine Negro pupils to Central High School. The others were assigned to the Negro high school.

Jefferson's father was a quiet, resourceful man. He had been employed by International Harvester for ten years. Jefferson's mother was a deeply religious woman who had implicit faith that the students would not suffer serious injuries.

Early in October, 1957, a small but well-organized group of segregationist students gained complete control inside the school. Significantly, it was about this time that the 101st Airborne troops were withdrawn from inside Central. They were replaced by the Arkansas federalized national guardsmen. The segregationist students were quick to note that, unlike the Army paratroopers, many of the guardsmen looked the other way when the Negro pupils were attacked.

The hoodlums used different methods of torture for each of the nine pupils. Each morning the gang would take up their stations at various points of the hallways. When Jeff would enter the corridor leading to his locker, one of them would yell, "Operation Fifteen!" It was the signal for one of the group wearing a black jacket and duck-tail haircut to slither up to Jeff and say, menacingly, "Nigger, ain't you scared?" Jeff would walk on, seemingly ignoring the thug, but at the same time warily scanning each group as he passed them along the corridors. He braced himself to "roll with the punch," as a fist was sure to shoot out from somewhere to strike him in the body.

One day after class Jeff and Terrance Roberts were descending the stairs near the office of the Vice-Principal of Girls, Mrs. Elizabeth Huckaby. The boys were in a good mood and talked of the party to be held at my home for them that weekend. Since they were near the Principal's office and soldiers were in the hall, they made the mistake of relaxing and letting their guard down. Two boys met them midway on the stairs, knocked the books from their hands, and kept moving.

As Jeff and Terrance stooped to pick up their scattered books, two other boys came up behind them and kicked them from the rear. Meanwhile, other boys started to play football, kicking the books around the floor.

Mrs. Huckaby heard the commotion and came outside to investigate. Seeing the attackers, she grabbed the first two offenders within her reach. The federalized national guardsmen, only six feet away, had witnessed the attack but stood smiling, making no effort to stop it or otherwise protect the Negro students.

The two boys who were apprehended by the Vice-Principal were given a three-day suspension. Two days after they returned to school, one of these boys hit Terrance while in gym class and threatened to beat him up after school that day. Later, in the afternoon, he kicked Carlotta Walls.

When the children reported these incidents to school authorities, they were told they would have to have an adult witness before any steps could be taken against the accused.

Several days later Jeff was standing at his locker watching two boys who were clowning around, pushing and shoving each other, as they approached him. He kept an eye on them, suspecting that they might push one or the other into him. As he watched, two other boys came up behind him. One of them struck him such a brutal blow behind his ear that Jeff was rendered unconscious. One of the teachers heard him fall in the hallway and came outside.

After reviving him, the teacher took him to the Principal's office. I was notified of the attack, and I immediately called Clarence Laws, Southwest Regional Field Secretary for the NAACP. He drove out to the school and took Jeff to the doctor. After the doctor treated Jefferson, they came to my house. When I saw the size of the lump on the side of Jeff's head I completely lost my temper. During my tirade against the school authorities for permitting this kind of cold-blooded cruelty to continue, I paused in front of Jeff, who sat huddled in a big chair. To my surprise he was smiling. This calmed me down somewhat. He said, "It's near suppertime. I better be getting home."

The next morning I telephoned his mother to inquire about his condition. She told me he felt better and that some of the swelling had left, but that the lump was still about the size of an egg. She said that Jeff was getting ready for school.

I cried, "Oh, no, he shouldn't go today!"

She said that she tried to persuade him to stay home, but he had told her, "No, if I stay out today, it'll be worse to-morrow."

After talking with Mrs. Thomas, I checked my daily rec-ords. The boy who attacked Jeff had been repeatedly reported to school authorities for hazing the Negro students.

At nine o'clock that morning, when Superintendent Blos-som arrived at his office, Clarence Laws and I were waiting to see him. We asked him what he intended to do about the continued brutal attacks on the children by the organized gang—attacks that had been reported many times. He said he was not aware of a large number of repeaters. We showed him the record of the pupils who had taken part in various attacks. As he looked at the long list of names and the repeated brutalities against the nine children, his expression lost some of its hardness, and his face seemed to soften. Momentarily there was no sign of the defiant attitude I had observed in him whenever anyone dared criticize him or his desegregation plan. Then as he straightened his shoulders, I said, "If you are really interested in clearing up this trouble, you should expel some of these repeated troublemakers."

He looked at me and blurted, "You can't tell me how to run my school."

"No, I can't," I retorted, "but it's up to you—not the Army —to maintain discipline inside the school. By not doing so, you are subjecting the children to physical torture that you will have to live with the rest of your life." As we left his office, I realized that we would have to seek help from some other source.

That afternoon I telephoned General Walker, the officer in command of the troops around the school, as I had done on many previous occasions, only to be told that he was not available. I called Thurgood Marshall in New York, and reported the attack on Jeff and our unsatisfactory conference with the School Superintendent. I also told him I had tried for weeks to get a conference with General Walker to see what could be done to lessen these attacks. Thurgood said he thought there was some kind of Army regulation which was possibly the reason the General could not talk with me. He said he would check at that end and see what could be done.

Meanwhile I called Val J. Washington, Director of the Minorities Division, Republican National Committee, in Washington, D.C., and told him about the attacks on the students, about our fruitless conference with the Superintendent of Schools, and our inability to talk with General Walker. I also pointed out that the lack of harmony between school authorities and the Army prevented the clearing up of the problem of discipline within the school. He said, "Keep the wire clear. I'll call you back shortly."

While waiting for his return call, Simeon Booker, a reporter with Johnson Publications in Chicago, came in. "Any news?" he inquired.

"Yes, but you can't print it," I answered. While discussing the events of the previous day, Val Washington called back and gave me the names of two of General Walker's aides whom I could contact, saying that they knew at all times how to reach the General.

Just as I finished talking to Val, the students arrived from school and told me what happened to them that day. Carlotta had been kicked, Melba had dropped her books in the hall and was kicked over on her face as she bent to pick them up; Ernest upon entering the shower room after gym class found the room so full of steam that he couldn't see and several boys threw hot, wet towels in his face; Elizabeth had signed out of school about three o'clock after girls in her gym class had hit her repeatedly with basketballs and the teacher had made no attempt to stop them; and the boys in Jeff's gym class had tried to push him into the hot steam pipes and had also deliberately knocked him down a number of times.

After the students left for home, I called one of General Walker's aides, who denied that he knew of the General's whereabouts. I said, "I have just received information from Washington that you and another aide know where the General is at all times. I want to talk to him immediately."

"I'll call you back," he said. While I waited for the call, Simeon typed up the list of that day's attacks against the children. When the aide called back, he asked if he could take my message for the General. After talking to him about five minutes, he realized the seriousness of my call and said, "Mrs. Bates, I think you should talk to General Walker. I'll have him call you." Shortly, General Walker telephoned. "Mrs. Bates, I understand you've been trying to get in touch with me."

"Yes, I've been trying to reach you by phone for weeks," I replied. I gave him a report of what had been happening to the students in the last three days. I pointed out that I was aware of the fact that it was not the job of the Army to discipline children inside the school, but that the children were not getting protection in the halls. At the end of our conversation, he said, "We'll take care of it."

Around nine thirty the next morning, Minnijean called me from the office of the Vice-Principal for Girls, saying, "Come and get us. We can't take it any longer. Melba and I are in Mrs. Huckaby's office. The junior mob has taken over the school. Jeff and Terry were attacked by a group of boys. They're in the office of the Vice-Principal for Boys. When we entered school this morning a boy wearing boots with steel taps on the toe kicked me. About five boys knocked Melba into her locker. We haven't seen the other kids since this morning."

I told Minnijean that they should remain in the office until I called. Evidently the news reached the Superintendent that the Negro pupils were planning to walk out because of lack of protection. For immediately after my telephone talk with Minnijean, Mr. Blossom called and said, "Try to encourage the students to remain. Additional guards are enroute to the school to provide adequate protection to the students."

At around 11:30 A.M., Carlotta called and said that two guards from the 101st Airborne had been assigned to each student. It was now quiet at the school.

Carlotta Walls

Carlotta Walls, a tenth grader, sat quietly beside me in the crowded courtroom. It was September 3, 1957, and we were listening attentively to the Court's proceedings as the attorneys for the school board petitioned the Federal Court for a delay in integration. We heard Judge Ronald N. Davies rule against the school board. He said he had read Mr. Faubus' speech in which the Governor had indicated that the troops were at the school only to maintain order and that they were neither integrationists nor segregationists. "I am taking these statements of the Governor at face value," Judge Davies declared. He ordered the school board "to put into effect forthwith" its plan of integration.

Thereupon, the school board immediately issued a statement that the schools would be opened the next morning to the Negro students. Carlotta asked me if I were going to notify the other pupils to be ready for school the next day.

I reminded her about the mob that was likely to face them, and asked, "Do you think they would want to go?"

"I'm sure most of them will," she said.

"And what about you?"

"Oh, I'll be there," she promised, "even if I have to go it alone."

Carlotta was fourteen. She was a tall, angular girl who liked swimming and bowling, and was one of the best baseball players in her neighborhood. She was the eldest of three daughters and lived with her parents, Mr. and Mrs. Cartelyou Walls, in a modern brick home in a quiet, integrated neighborhood.

Her father, a brick mason by trade, served three years in the Army during World War II. Two of these years were spent in the Pacific with the 477th Anti-Aircraft Coast Artillery. He was awarded two battle stars and a Philippine decoration for bravery in action.

Carlotta's pretty, thirty-two-year-old mother, Mrs. Juanita Walls, worked as a secretary in the office of a public housing project. After work Mrs. Walls usually stopped at my home to pick up Carlotta who visited me at the close of school each day. One afternoon Mrs. Walls told me, "I try not to let Carlotta know how much I worry. I can't say that I'm not proud of her. Sometimes she gets impatient with me when she's talking about what's happening at Central. And I'd say, 'Now, Carlotta, it can't be that bad.' Little does she realize that every time I see a bruise on her leg where some bully has kicked her with steel tips on his shoes, I'm just about ready to commit murder. I keep thinking each day, maybe tomorrow it won't be her leg; it will be her eye."

Such was the courage of the parents—smiling while their hearts were breaking. Nevertheless, Mrs. Walls could not hide her worry entirely. For before school ended eight months later, this young mother's hair had turned almost white.

Carlotta was subjected to much the same type of physical and psychological tortures as the other students.

Each day after school I sat with the embattled nine in the quiet basement of my home, away from the probing eyes of the reporters and the hysterical charges by the segregationists that the pupils were hirelings of the NAACP, imported from the North to integrate "our" schools.

131

These meetings were not unlike group therapy. In relating the day's experiences, all the suppressed emotions within these children came tumbling out.

Carlotta would pace the floor, saying, "If only I could sock her!" She was referring to one of her classmates who followed her constantly in the halls, stepping on her heels and calling her names. After school one day, Carlotta was delivered to my house as usual under escort of a guardsman. She stopped off at my kitchen to fix herself a ham sandwich before joining the other children in the basement for our daily session. She came down the stairs holding a grape soda in one hand and the sandwich in the other.

"I'm sorry to hold up the meeting," she announced, sheepishly. "I didn't have any lunch." Then she explained: "When I left my classroom before lunch, *that* girl was waiting for me. One of my teachers joined me and walked to the cafeteria with me. Just as I started to eat my lunch, the girl passed my table and dropped a handful of milk bottle tops and soiled paper napkins in my food. I almost hit her!" She pointed her finger at me and added emotionally, "I don't care what you say. One of these days I'm going to knock the hell out of her!"

A few days later Carlotta related another incident. "Today I was walking down the hall. In fact I was nearly running. *That* girl was trying to keep up with me. I turned suddenly and stepped on her foot. But hard! I smiled at her and called her a few choice names, and I told her what I'd do to her if she didn't leave me alone. And each time I saw her after that, I smiled, pretty like. And you know what? She didn't come near me anymore today."

Carlotta ended her story thus: "You know, today was rather a nice day at school."

Elizabeth Eckford

Elizabeth Eckford a fifteen-year-old, strong-willed adolescent, meant business about going to Central. As described earlier in these pages, Elizabeth suffered most at the hands of the mob. Yet she complained the least.

She lived with her family in a modern six-room bungalow on the west side of town. Her father, Oscar Eckford, worked nights as a dining car maintenance worker. He was employed by the Missouri Pacific Railroad and worked at the Little Rock railroad station. Elizabeth's mother, Mrs. Birdie Eckford, was a plump, warm, sentimental person whose strength of character seemed to engulf her family.

Elizabeth was next to the eldest of six children. Her first major battle with her family was over the issue of going to Central. Around the first of August, 1957, a month before school was to open, Elizabeth told her mother she wanted to attend Central and asked that she go with her to the office of the school board and request a transfer. Her mother said, "All right, we'll go one day." Her mother was hoping she would forget about it. Two weeks passed before Elizabeth mentioned it again. Near the end of August, Elizabeth became more determined. She faced her mother again. "We're going to the school board office and we're going today," she pressed.

Mrs. Eckford told me later, "I knew it was useless to argue with her, so we went to the office of the School Superintendent, and she was admitted."

Elizabeth's stay at Central could be called anything but pleasant. However, the months of harassment were somewhat assuaged by the mounds of letters from all over the world that arrived for her at my home each day. After separating the foreign mail from the domestic mail, Elizabeth would carefully place the stamps in a box to be salvaged later for her stamp collection. She would then bounce out of my house, saying, "I've got to do my homework and finish a dress for school tomorrow."

Thelma Mothershed

Thelma Mothershed, a sixteen-year-old eleventh grader, was just over five feet tall. She scarcely weighed ninety-five pounds. She was the only one of the nine students who was born outside of the city of Little Rock. Her parents, Mr. and Mrs. A. L. Mothershed, came up from Texas and settled in Little Rock when Thelma was three years old.

Thelma's parents were alarmed when she told them she wanted to attend Central High School. And understandably so, for Thelma had been afflicted with a cardiac condition since infancy. While in elementary school she had to be tutored at home for three years. When she finished junior high, her mother tried in vain to talk Thelma out of enrolling at Central. The situation called for a family conference. Thelma's two older sisters, Lois, twenty, a music student at Phillips University in Enid, Oklahoma, the first Negro to attend the university, and her eighteen-year-old sister Grace, who was attending the University of Arkansas, came home for the conference. When the conference was over, Thelma's wishes prevailed. She was going to attend Central High School. Her mother took the frail but determined Thelma to the office of the school board and requested a transfer from Horace Mann, the Negro high school, to Central.

Mr. Mothershed, who was employed as a psychiatric aide at the Veterans' Hospital, told me later, "I agreed with her mother that the physical plant at Central probably wouldn't be good for Thelma—climbing stairs and so on. But I was secretly pulling for her, and I was proud when she stood up to us and won."

Thelma suffered a mild heart attack on the first day the students went into Central under the protection of the city police. That afternoon Carlotta confided to me, "I don't think Thelma wants you to know she had an attack this morning. It happened while we were being shown around the school. She was carried into someone's office while we kept going on the tour."

On hearing the news I immediately informed Mrs. Mothershed of what had happened. I fully expected her to say that Thelma would have to withdraw. I had recently heard that an Oklahoma minister of Mrs. Mothershed's church had been reading about Thelma in the newspapers and had offered her a scholarship in an integrated high school in his city. And so I suggested that perhaps Mrs. Mothershed and her husband should consider the scholarship offer made by the minister. The mother was firm in her reply. "No," she said, "indeed not. Thelma has made up her mind. What I will do is contact the school authorities and see if they can arrange Thelma's classes so she won't have to climb so many stairs."

If one wanted to strain a point to be charitable, he could point out that the segregationists must have had a spark of decency in them after all. For as it turned out they harassed Thelma less than they did the other pupils. Of course, when they made a desperate effort at one time to discourage the students from returning after the Christmas holidays,

Thelma was kicked and shoved along with the other Negro youngsters and knocked flat on her face on the metal stairs.

In spite of her illness, Thelma had a near perfect record for attendance in her year at Central. She and the other Negro students received awards from many organizations throughout the country. The awards were tantamount to recognition for courage on a field of battle.

Three days after school closed I accompanied the children on a flight to Chicago to receive the Robert S. Abbott Civil Rights Award. It was presented by John H. Sengstacke, publisher of the *Chicago Defender*. We then flew on to New York to receive a similar award from the Hotel and Club Employees Union, Local 6, AFL-CIO.

The trip to New York was filled with excitement, yet all the time the children were aware that this was no mere happy excursion and that their mission was indeed a serious one. Still they were hailed as heroes everywhere in the city. They dined with the then Governor Averell Harriman, and were received at New York's City Hall by Mayor Robert F. Wagner. They went to the museums, the parks and the zoos. And of course there was a visit to the Statue of Liberty. Thelma could not join the others in climbing their way up the stairs of the huge statue. While waiting for her colleagues, she stood inside the pedestal and read the immortal poem of Emma Lazarus engraved on a tablet.

"I've read it many times before in print," she told me. "But reading it now is much more meaningful to me." She now read the words aloud:

> Not like the brazen giant of Greek fame,
> With conquering limbs astride from land to land;
> Here at our sea-washed, sunset gates shall stand
> A mighty woman with a torch, whose flame

Is the imprisoned lightning, and her name
Mother of Exiles. From her beacon-hand
Glows world-wide welcome; her mild eyes command
The air-bridged harbor that twin cities frame.
"Keep, ancient lands, your storied pomp!" cries she
With silent lips. "Give me your tired, your poor,
Your huddled masses yearning to breathe free,
The wretched refuse of your teeming shore.
Send these, the homeless, tempest-tost to me,
I lift my lamp beside the golden door!"

The next day, as the children were being honored by the
Reverend Gardner Taylor and his congregation at the Concord Baptist Church in Brooklyn, Thelma suffered an attack
and collapsed. The constant day-by-day strain of her experience at Central High, followed by the excitement of the New
York events, had been too much for her.

After Thelma received medical attention, I flew home with
her. She spent most of the summer in the hospital under the
care of a heart specialist. When she was discharged from the
hospital, the doctor told her to "take it easy" and that she
would be all right. Her mother said, "I'll see to that!" For
Thelma this meant that rock 'n' roll was out of her life for
a while. Mrs. Mothershed saw to that, too.

Thelma said, "Okay, Mother. Rock 'n' roll isn't all that
important." What mattered most to Thelma was whether
she could return to Central. She told me that when she asked
the doctor about this, he sat looking at her for a while, then
said, "I don't see any reason why you can't."

As she talked, I was reminded of the words of the late
Judge Learned Hand: "Liberty lies in the hearts of men and
women; when it dies there, no constitution, no law, no court
can save it."

I looked at Thelma and thought these words might have been written about her.

Terrance Roberts

Terrance Roberts, a fifteen-year-old, soft-spoken, diligent student was next to the eldest of seven children of Mr. and Mrs. William H. Roberts.

Mr. Roberts, a World War II Naval veteran, worked in the Dietetics Department at the Veterans' Hospital in North Little Rock. Mrs. Roberts operated a catering service from her home.

Terrance, like Jeff, was subjected to cruelties that ordinarily would break the spirit of most fifteen-year-olds. But Terrance had made his decision and he was sticking by it. Only once did he threaten to quit. It was on the afternoon of February 4, 1958, when Terrance said to me, "I've had it! Today, during the eighth period in the study hall, two boys kicked me. One was the same boy who kicked Jeff last week. When I reported them to the office of the Vice-Principal, I was asked if a teacher or an adult saw them kick me. We've reported one of these boys many times. Now the school authorities are telling us that unless we have an adult witness nothing will be done no matter what they do to us."

I made no effort to influence Terrance to continue at Central. I told him, "If you should decide not to go back, I will understand."

The next morning Terrance was one of the first of the nine to arrive at Central. That afternoon I asked him what made him change his mind. "I thought about it last night and decided I wasn't going to let that little pip-squeak chase me out of Central." Overnight Terrance had regained his courage.

Melba Pattillo

Melba Patillo, a fifteen-year-old, poised, talented, and articulate youngster, has wanted to be an actress as long as she could remember. Her mother, Mrs. Lois Pattillo, a teacher, tried to help Melba realize her ambition by making it possible for her to begin at an early age to study ballet, voice, and piano.

Melba lived with her mother and thirteen-year-old brother, Conrad, who was Melba's "Number One" fan. Mrs. Pattillo taught English at Jones High School in North Little Rock.

Melba suffered much the same assortment of indignities as were visited on the other students. Fortunately, she was able to absorb the abuse and taunting without serious damage to her personality.

Gloria Ray

Gloria Ray had just turned fifteen when she entered Central High School. She lived with her parents, Mr. and Mrs. Harvey C. Ray, in a two-story white colonial house. Gloria was the youngest of three children. Mrs. Ray was a social worker employed by the Department of Welfare in Little Rock. She was a serious-minded, pleasant person who supported wholeheartedly the course of action of her young daughter in the Central High School issue.

Mr. Ray, in his late sixties, was forced to retire from work in 1953 on account of a heart condition. He had been employed as an Agricultural Agent for the Arkansas State Department of Agriculture. Mr. Ray did not always fathom all the new ideas of his "baby," as he referred to Gloria. Nor could he understand why she wanted to be a "crusader."

Nevertheless, he, along with his wife, gave Gloria whole-hearted support.

Gloria was a slender, attractive girl with a charming personality. She also knew how to get her way with her parents. She was an above-average student who planned to enter on a career in science.

One evening Gloria told her mother that Ernest Green and some of her other friends were going to Central to register the next day, and that she wanted to go with them. It was the final day of registration. She asked if she could use the family car. Gloria had indicated to her parents three months earlier, in May, when she was graduated from junior high school, that she wanted to attend Central. At that time Mrs. Ray saw no objection to the plan. However, the next morning she reconsidered. "You know," she said to Gloria, "there has been a lot of talk by the segregationists about not wanting Negroes at Central. If there is trouble it would be hard on your father with his heart condition. Don't you think it would be wiser if you forgot about Central and registered at Horace Mann High School instead?"

Gloria said she'd think about it.

That night Mrs. Ray asked Gloria if she had registered at school.

"Yes, I sure did," Gloria said.

"Where? At which school?"

"At Central, of course," said Gloria matter-of-factly.

"But hadn't we talked about your registering at Horace Mann?"

"Yes, I know," Gloria said. "But Central is so much closer and I didn't see why I should drive all the way across town to Horace Mann. So I registered with Ernest and the other kids at Central."

"Well," declared Mrs. Ray, "maybe we shouldn't tell Dad about it yet—not at this time."

"But, Mother, we can't keep it from him," Gloria protested. "He has to know about it some time."

"I'll find a way to tell him," Mrs. Ray said.

On the morning of September 4, when Elizabeth and the other students were under attack by the mob and were being turned back by the guardsmen, Mr. Ray was tuned in on a television news program. He heard the newscaster say that nine Negro pupils were being turned away from Central High School and that one of the girls was surrounded by a mob. The commentator gave the names of the students who had been admitted to Central. Mr. Ray was to learn for the first time that his "baby," Gloria, was one of the nine.

In the weeks that followed, when the students were kept out of school by the National Guard, Mr. Ray offered to send Gloria to any private school of her choice. Gloria told me later, "I told Dad that I loved him dearly and I certainly would not do anything to impair his health. But quit Central, no. That was something that I could not do."

When Mr. Ray realized that it was impossible to discourage Gloria, he told me, "I know I shall be terrified each day, each hour she's at Central. But I'm proud she has the courage to do it."

Although Gloria was subjected to a certain amount of physical abuse, the attacks on her were mostly of a psychological nature. A few days before the Christmas holidays, a girl sitting next to her in her homeroom told her that she had heard that some of the boys had guns in school that day. Later, Gloria was walking down the corridor of the second floor when torpedoes—a type of firecracker—started exploding around her.

141

She said that afternoon, "When I heard the first explosion, I was so frightened I couldn't move. I was sure they were shooting at me." She added, "I saw the guardsmen take a boy who was dropping the torpedoes to the Principal's office."

The next day a boy attempted to lasso Gloria with a rope fashioned into a hangman's noose. The threat to hang Gloria was followed up by a phone call to her mother that evening. The unidentified caller told Mrs. Ray, "If Gloria comes to school tomorrow there will be a lynching."

The psychological and physical attacks continued in the vain effort to break the spirit of the students. Under these attacks the seeds of freedom that were planted deep in the hearts of these youngsters began to sprout, grow, and develop into a force that was to have far-reaching effects in the continuing struggle for first-class citizenship.

Just before the spring vacation in 1958, as the children were leaving Central, the segregationists spread a rumor around the campus that some of the boys were going to bring water pistols filled with acid to school the next day and spray the liquid on the Negro students. Gloria was informed about this by a so-called "friend" and advised that it would probably be better if she stayed home the next day.

Gloria did not tell me or her parents about the threat.

The next morning Mrs. Ray stood on the porch and watched her daughter join the other students in the carpool that transported them each day to and from school.

The carpool plan was instituted after school authorities felt it was no longer necessary for the federalized national guardsmen to transport the children to school. Because teen-age gangs constantly roved around the vicinity of Central looking for an opportunity to strike out at the students, the Negro parents agreed that the carpool plan was essential for protection of their children. Even so, on several occasions their cars were stoned and the windows smashed.

When Gloria waved to her mother as they were driving off that morning, Mrs. Ray said, "God keep them safe today."

Immediately after the students drove off, Mrs. Ray phoned me to tell me about the phone call she had received the night before.

"I received a call around midnight," she related. "It was a woman who said that her son attended Central and that he had heard that some of the boys would have water pistols loaded with acid the next day. The woman said that, as a parent herself, she felt it was her duty to warn me about the danger to my daughter. And, the woman said, 'If I were you I'd keep my daughter at home.'"

Mrs. Ray went on: "I tried to reason that this was only a new form of intimidation they were trying. But how can I live with the possibility that the woman could be telling the truth, that acid might be thrown in my child's face, possibly blinding her for life. There was no sleep for me last night."

By the time I was able to reach the Vice-Principal by phone, the damage had been done. When Elizabeth was entering her homeroom, someone squirted ink on the back of her dress. She had spent precious hours making the garment. As Gloria was leaving her locker, she saw a group of boys blocking the hall. She recognized them to be among the troublemakers. She turned and walked in the opposite direction. Just as she turned a corner in the corridor, she came face to face with a boy holding a water pistol. He aimed it at her face.

She told me later, "If I live forever I don't think I'll ever be as frightened as I was at that moment. I just stood there, petrified with fear. I shut my eyes tight. After liquid hit me in the face, I could hear the boy running down the hall. I dropped my books and grabbed the hem of my dress and wiped my face. It took a moment or so before I could convince myself that it was only water." As Gloria was relating this horrifying experience, tears came rolling down her cheeks, but she was apparently unaware that she was crying.

In spite of the mounting attacks, the incessant humiliations, the degradations, and the harassments inflicted on the Negro students, the courageous youngsters were not to be deterred from their single-minded goal. When school reconvened after spring vacation, all of them returned to their classes at Central. And when they did, the harassments resumed.

One day Gloria started on her way down from the third floor of Central High School. She had taken only a few steps down the flight of steel stairs when she heard a woman's scream from behind her. Gloria quickly connected the scream with some impending danger to herself. And she was right.

A boy had silently been following her down the stairway. He was about to lunge at her to push her down the flight of steps. The scream had alerted Gloria to the attack from behind. Without turning around, she immediately ran down the stairs, gripping the tubular railing for support. When the boy caught up with her, he bumped her so hard she momentarily lost her breath while he sped on. Having braced herself against the railing, Gloria remained on her feet.

Many of the teachers—particularly the younger ones—did everything within their power to protect the nine students. Some went out of their way to help the students catch up with work they had missed when they were barred from entering the school in the first weeks of the term. Concerned over the lack of protection given the Negro students within the school, the teachers took it upon themselves to oversee the hallways in between class breaks. In this way they attempted to discourage the segregationist students from tormenting the Negro children.

One of the teachers had been standing in the doorway of her classroom looking down the stairway. It was she who had witnessed the attack on Gloria and had screamed the alert.

Ernest Green

Ernest Green was the only senior among the nine Negro students at Little Rock's Central High School. At age sixteen, he showed maturity beyond his years. Since the death in 1953 of his father, a World War I veteran, Ernest had assumed the position of head of the household. His mother, kindly and soft-spoken, was an elementary-school teacher. Both she and Ernest's fourteen-year-old brother, Scott, respected his status as head of the family. Ernest possessed level judgment, and he never seemed to become ruffled. He always carried about him an air of calm assurance.

Mrs. Green told me one day, "When Ernest announced to the family that he was going to enroll at Central, we knew it was useless to try to talk him out of it. I only pointed out the difficulty in changing schools in his senior year. The adjustment not only to a new school but to different children would not be easy, I told him. But I left the decision to him."

Ernest's aunt, Mrs. Treopia Gravely, was a teacher at Horace Mann High School. She told Ernest, "If you really want to go to Central High, we will stand behind you. If you have faith in what you are doing and the courage of your convictions, we'll help you see it through. It won't be easy, but once you enter there'll be no turning back."

Mrs. Green had no idea at the time of the mental and

physical violence that was to be inflicted on Ernest for the entire year. "Each day I pray for Ernest's safety," she once told me, "and for personal courage to withstand the agonizing fears that plague us."

In many ways it was harder on the parents than on the children. Ernest's mother was typical of the other Negro parents. Not knowing what was happening to their children in school or what was going to happen that night or the next day was not the least of the tortures which the parents were forced to endure.

Mrs. Green told me, "I can always tell at a glance when Ernest comes home from school whether he had a bad day—even though he always tries to hide it. He nearly always comes in with a smile or he tells a joke in his nonchalant way. I remember shortly after the second school term began, Ernest came home one day furiously angry. He said that two boys who had been making trouble the entire term had viciously attacked him that day. I tried to be strong and not show any sympathy on my face because I could see he was at the breaking point. In a calm voice, which was far from my feeling, I asked, 'Are you hurt?' He said, 'No, but it makes me so mad that those morons continue to pick on us time and again and nothing is done about it.' I asked him to tell me what happened. He said, 'Carlotta and I had just finished eating lunch today and were going up the steps when a boy tried to trip Carlotta. She twisted aside, causing him to fall. Then a friend of this boy, who is nearly always with the gang, rushed up the steps behind me and hit me twice on the jaw. As soon as he clouted me, he ran down the steps, but I chased after him and told a guardsman about it. The boy tried to get away. He ran outside the school and attempted to sneak into the cafeteria through the back door, but the officer caught him and I identified him to a sergeant of the guards.' "

On several occasions when I met with the children at my home, the strain of the day's events had proved too much for some of the girls to relate without tears. Ernest would snap them out of it with a few words, sometimes serious, sometimes flippant, depending on what the particular situation called for. When the other children dwelt on the brutal acts inflicted on them that day, Ernest would manage somehow to change the subject and get them to talk about something else. Many times I saw him hide his own anger and fear so as to encourage the others. And despite the days when his own face was lined with fatigue, he seemed miraculously to regain his composure as soon as he joined the other children.

If Ernest could experience anger and fear, he could also feel hurt. And few incidents pained him as much as his being told he could not play tenor sax with the school band. Ernest was, in fact, a talented musician with the saxophone. However, he passed it off with a wry attempt at being funny. "They are denying the world another 'Bird' Parker," he said.

Around the first of May, 1958, a few weeks before graduation, Ernest took me aside. Out of earshot of the other students, he said, "Mrs. Bates, do you know whether the police or the National Guard will be at our graduation?" Both his question and tone of voice were disquieting.

"Are things getting worse in school?" I asked him.

"No," he said. "Things have been kind of quiet the last few days. But today everyone is saying I won't be allowed to march with the graduating class. They say it like boasting. I don't know if it's true or not."

I had an appointment in Washington the following week and I told Ernest I would try to see someone in the office of the Secretary of the Army at the Pentagon about providing adequate protection at graduation.

The day I was to go to the Pentagon, Secretary of the Army Wilbur M. Brucker was testifying before a Congressional Committee. I therefore couldn't get to see him. Since I could not remain over until the next day, I handled the matter with one of the Secretary's aides who was close to the Little Rock troop situation.

Earlier, I visited the office of Congressman Brooks Hays of Arkansas' Fifth District, which included Little Rock. Congressman Hays and I discussed what was happening to the students inside Central. He seemed extremely depressed over the turn of events since September but praised the nine students for the "sane and dignified way in which they conducted themselves during a very difficult situation."

I told him of my proposed visit to the Pentagon. He said, "I'm sure after talking to you they will recognize the gravity of the situation." He offered his help in any way that he could.

The Secretary's aide was well aware of the actions of the small group of organized segregationist students inside the school. His office had already criticized the school board for permitting this small group to terrorize the Negro students.

Before I left the office of the Secretary of the Army, I was assured that protection would be provided.

Baccalaureate services preceding the graduation ceremonies were held at Central High School on May 25, 1958. Ernest Green marched with the 602-member graduating class onto the field of Quigley Stadium. On hand were 125 federalized Arkansas national guardsmen along with numerous city police and detectives. Central High School's first integrated baccalaureate service was now in progress.

Superintendent Virgil Blossom refused to allow Negro reporters, including Sarah Slack of the *New York Amsterdam News,* and Simeon Booker and Ernest Withers of the Johnson Publications of Chicago, to cover the proceedings. He did not want anything to interfere with the "dignity" of the occasion, he told them. In the press box were white reporters and television cameramen. I arranged for Sarah Slack to attend the ceremony as a guest of the Green family in another section of the field.

The hour-long services ended without incident. But as the crowd of twenty-five hundred was leaving the stadium, a member of the graduating class, Curtis E. Stover, jumped off a near by embankment and spat in the face of a Negro girl.

Police Chief Eugene Smith, who had been walking a few paces behind the girl and her friends, immediately arrested the boy.

The *Arkansas Gazette* gave the following account of the incident on the next day:

> The spitting incident, which passed unnoticed by most of the crowd, occurred as the Negroes were walking to the taxis.
>
> Police Chief Eugene G. Smith said that he and Capt. R. E. Brians were walking a few paces behind some Negro girls when the Stover youth, a member of the graduating class, jumped off a nearby ledge and spit in the face of one of the girls.
>
> Smith instructed Brians to get the girls out of the way and he arrested Stover and turned him over to a police officer.
>
> The youth was standing in a crowd of policemen on Sixteenth Street just outside the Stadium when a girl, later identified as one of his sisters, began crying and shouting at the officers.
>
> Then Stover's mother, Mrs. Elsie Marie Stover, arrived and started talking to the officers. O. D. Gunter, a photographer for the Arkansas Democrat, made a picture and Mrs. Stover

protested vehemently. She picked up a wooden "No Parking" sign that had been placed near the curb and swung it at Gunter, but he ducked and a policeman took the sign away from her.

Then a police patrol car arrived. Mrs. Margaret C. Jackson, president of the segregationalist League of Central High Mothers, and Mrs. Stover, a member of the League, got in the car first, followed by the youth and several officers.

They were taken to the police station where the youth was booked. Then Mrs. Stover fainted and her two daughters, Marie, 15, and Anita, 17, screamed.

The youth walked away from the police officers at that point and one officer yelled at other policemen to stop him. The two girls then started kicking at the officers and screaming.

The police called an ambulance for Mrs. Stover but when it arrived she refused to get in it and later left with Mrs. Jackson.

The two girls were placed in juvenile detention quarters but were released after about 10 minutes with instructions to appear in Court this morning.

On May 27, 1958, Ernest Green, dressed in black cap and gown, was handed a diploma. He became the first Negro graduate in the history of Central High School in Little Rock. According to an estimate publicized by the segregationists, Ernest's diploma cost taxpayers approximately $5,000,000.

On the following morning the graduates returned to the school to receive their final grades. One of Ernest's classmates waved to him and called from across the campus, "Wish you luck, Green!"

Ernest smiled and waved back.

The next day saw the school term come to a close, and the more than four hundred federalized national guardsmen, on the order of President Eisenhower, vacated the premises.

Whether the troops would return in the fall when school was to reopen was anybody's guess. Officially there was only silence. Those who were fearful about the future of the Negro students at Central placed their hopes on newspaper reports that said that United States Marshals would be on hand to protect the students in September. But officially there was only more silence.

Shortly before the school year ended, the Little Rock School Board petitioned the Federal District Court for a delay in integration at Central High School. It asked that the Negro pupils currently enrolled be removed and that integration be postponed until the January mid-term of 1961. A hearing was held in mid-June and the NAACP attorneys were on hand to oppose the petition. Presiding Judge Harry J. Lemley granted the school board's request for a delay. The NAACP attorneys immediately appealed the decision.

While we waited for the result, the segregationists kept busy. On July 10 the following item appeared in the newspapers across the nation:

MRS. L. C. BATES
HANGED IN EFFIGY

Camden, July 10 (AP)—An effigy of Mrs. L. C. Bates, president of the Arkansas branch of the National Association for the Advancement of Colored People, was found hanging from a tree on the Ouachita County Courthouse lawn tonight.

Deputy Sheriff Charles Gillespie said a sign that hung across the effigy's chest read "Old Daisy Bates—Ike's Best Friend."

Gillespie said it was the second effigy of Mrs. Bates found

here in two days. He said he removed one Wednesday from a rural mailbox.

The second effigy had a face made of a rubber mask and was dressed in hoop skirts. It was found by passersby about 10 P.M., Gillespie said.

The next week Governor Faubus won the Democratic nomination, tantamount to election in Arkansas, for a third term. His victory was by an overwhelming majority.

In August the United States Eighth Circuit Court of Appeals, in a six-to-one ruling, reversed the decision of Judge Lemley. As an observation, it is worth noting that the lone dissenter was Chief Judge Archibald K. Gardner, of Heron, South Dakota, then reported to be ninety years old and the oldest active judge in the nation. The majority opinion was written by Judge Martin C. Matthes, then fifty-two, and the youngest judge on the Eighth United States Circuit Court bench.

The majority opinion stated in part: "... We say that the time has not yet come in the United States when an order of a Federal Court must be whittled away, watered down, or shamefully withdrawn in the face of violent and unlawful acts of individual citizens in opposition thereto..."

However, the Court granted the school board a stay of execution to allow time for an appeal to the Supreme Court.

On August 26 Governor Faubus addressed an Extraordinary Session of the State Legislature in which he recommended a "package" of segregation bills for its consideration. In his speech the Governor said:

... When it comes to a decision by the head of the state upon a matter involving its life, the ordinary rights of individuals must yield to what he deems the necessities of the moment. Public danger warrants the substitution of executive process

152

for judicial process ... Gentlemen, may I say to you in the deepest humility and sincerity that it is with exceeding regret that I have determined this extraordinary session of the Legislature to be necessary.

We must do whatever is possible to protect the rights of our people, and preserve for them and their posterity, the democratic processes of government which we all cherish so much.

This battle for States' Rights and Constitutional Government is not of our choosing, as has been the case many times in the history of the past; the issue has been forced upon us and we must either choose to defend our rights against those who would usurp them, or else surrender.

We, as public servants, elected by the vote of our people, would be unworthy of the confidence reposed in us, and of the honor bestowed upon us, should we be unwilling to face the issue as free men should, and do everything in our power that is possible to be done.

I hope that no one of you will be influenced by the words of the weak and the fearful, and that no one of you will be misled by the mistaken views of those who would surrender all the rights and privileges we have enjoyed, to an all-powerful federal government in the unwise course of action which it pursues at the present moment. The issues which must be faced and decided by free men have never been easy, and the tasks which must be performed by a people who would remain free, have always been difficult.

This is not a half serious problem, and it cannot be met with half measures. The bills I have recommended to you are the product of many fine and able minds, and represent a great deal of hard work. I ask that you consider these measures as a package program ...

The text of the school-closing law read, in part, as follows:

AN ACT to Provide the Procedure Under Which the Governor May Order to Be Closed the Schools of Any School District; and for Other Purposes.

Be it enacted by the General Assembly of the State of Arkansas:

SECTION 1. The Governor shall, by proclamation filed with the Secretary of State, and with the Board of Directors, of any school district affected, and with the County Board of Election Commissioners of the appropriate county:

(A) Order any school or all schools of the district to be closed immediately, and he is hereby specifically empowered to use all forces at his command to execute such order; and

(B) Call a special election to be held in the school district within thirty (30) days thereafter, whenever

(a) He shall determine that in order to maintain the peace against actual or impending domestic violence in any public school district, whereof the lives or limbs of the citizens, students, teachers or other employees of any school, or the safety of buildings or other property in the school district are endangered, he (the Governor) may, acting in his discretion, order any school in the district to be closed . . .

The United States Supreme Court heard oral arguments for three and one-half hours on September 11, on whether the eight Negro youngsters should be permitted to return to Central High School. Thurgood Marshall, in his closing plea, asked the Court to decide the case "in such a fashion as to make it clear to the politicians in Arkansas that the Constitution means what it says."

The next day, the nine Supreme Court Justices made it clear, not only to the Arkansas politicians but to the world, that the Constitution meant what it said. In this historic session they decreed in a unanimous decision that integration must proceed immediately at Central High School, no matter how violent the opposition.

Upon hearing the news, Governor Faubus immediately signed the "package" of segregation bills passed at the Extraordinary Legislative Session and ordered Little Rock's three white and one Negro high school closed. The four schools shut down were: Central High School, Hall High School, Technical High School, and the all-Negro Horace Mann High School. The Governor later explained at a press conference that he was closing the schools because he had determined that "domestic violence is impending if Negroes were admitted to Central."

With thousands of pupils barred from the high schools by the Governor's Proclamation, the hate campaign was intensified. Segregationists, masterful in their tactics at distortion, now claimed that the Negroes were responsible for the closing of the schools. Governor Faubus, in his finest rhetoric, declared: "If Daisy Bates would find an honest job and go to work, and if the U.S. Supreme Court would keep its cotton-picking hands off the Little Rock School Board's affairs, we could open the Little Rock (public) schools!"

On September 17 a new group appeared on the scene under the name of the Save Our Schools Committee. The following statement issued by the Committee appeared in the *Arkansas Democrat:*

Governor Faubus can't help us because he has a mandate from the people to stop forced integration and stop violence. (Faubus believes that the people make the law of the land.)

The federal government can't help us because they have a mandate from the NAACP to force this on us even with tanks, guns and bayonets.

If we can appeal to the parents of the seven children and Mrs. Bates and keep all outsiders out who started this thing, we can solve this problem in a Christian way with a little time. But force will not work; we freedom-loving, God-fearing American people will not bow down by force from anyone. Hitler, nor Hirohito could not make us knuckle under and neither can the NAACP.

We shall and will continue to help our neighbors and brothers in a Christian way, but force never. The Communist and NAACP policy is divide and conquer; this is their first step.

A series of advertisements appeared in the same newspaper. One of them addressed to Negro ministers and educators, read as follows:

A SPECIAL MESSAGE
ADDRESSED TO THE FOLLOWING
COLORED CITIZENS OF ARKANSAS

Dr. Lafayette Harris,
   President of Philander Smith College
Dr. J. M. Robinson,
   An outstanding doctor—leader and builder
Bishop Sherman
Reverend Guy
Reverend Roland Smith
Reverend Charles Walker
Reverend Harry Bass
All of whom are outstanding Christian Ministers.

Dr. Harris, you are well aware of the fine cooperation which has always existed in Little Rock between the races. With your great leadership, we (both white and colored) have built one of the outstanding colleges in the country.

This message is addressed to you and is being published in the press because you as leaders in your respective fields enjoy the respect and confidence of the people of your race as well as the white citizens of our state.

Individually and collectively, you can make a great contribution and perform an important service in behalf of all citizens of our state in this grave situation which has developed.

Until a year ago, the relations existing between the colored and white citizens of Arkansas were harmonious and pleasant. Each race respected and had confidence in each other.

Down through the years, the colored and white citizens of Arkansas have accomplished much together for the good and improvement of all.

The key to the present grave situation which has developed and exists at this time, is in the hands of your race, the parents of the seven colored children and Mrs. L. C. Bates. The Federal Government, State Government and City Government have failed to furnish the leadership in this great crisis. As citizens of Arkansas and as leaders of your race, you are urged to counsel with those who direct the activities of the N.A.A.C.P. in Arkansas—parents of the children, recommend and urge that they be tolerant and not press their position too strongly at this critical time. Instead, we urge you to induce the seven colored children to wait and give both you and us a chance to work this out in a peaceable manner. With time, we pledge with your help, we will solve this great problem.

SAVE OUR SCHOOLS COMMITTEE
I. Smith, Secretary

Smaller advertisements were addressed to leading white ministers. The following messages were typical:

BISHOP ROBERT R. BROWN

A trip to Washington won't help. Please appeal to Mrs. Bates and seven parents to give us time to accept this change in a Christian manner. Mrs. Bates holds the key.

SAVE OUR SCHOOLS COMMITTEE
I. Smith, Secretary

BISHOP PAUL E. MARTIN—

Please for all Christian people (white and colored) appeal to Mrs. Bates and 7 parents to give us time and with men like you leading the way we can and will accept this change in a Christian way. Force and violence is not the way.

157

SAVE OUR SCHOOLS COMMITTEE
I. Smith, Secretary

PREACHER DALE COWLING:

You and your ministerial alliance please pray for Mrs. Bates and the seven parents to please give our Christian, law abiding citizens a chance to accept this philosophy in a christian-like manner and not try to force us.

SAVE OUR SCHOOLS COMMITTEE
I. Smith, Secretary

A separate advertisement was aimed at parents and teachers in these words:

PARENTS AND TEACHERS—

(Both white and colored) Please get petitions, rallys and prayer meetings started to appeal to Mrs. Bates and the seven parents to give us time and we will help solve our problem in a Christian way, not by force, hate and violence. They hold the key.

SAVE OUR SCHOOLS COMMITTEE
I. Smith, Secretary

On September 18 I was driving home from the *State Press*. About six blocks from my home a car suddenly crashed into the rear of my car. I stopped, and in the rearview mirror I could see three boys in the car that had struck mine. One of them leaned out of the car window. "Get out of our way!" he ordered.

To avoid any "incidents," I drove on. They followed close behind, shouting insults and profanities along the way. I took a small automatic from the glove compartment of the car and laid it in my lap. When I was forced to stop at an intersection, they pulled up alongside me. A boy in the back seat jumped out of the car and came up to my open car window, shaking his fist and cursing. "You and those damn coons are responsible for the closing of our school!" he yelled at me.

I made no reply. Just stared at him. He continued ranting and cursing. "I ought to pull you out of that car and beat you to a pulp!" he snarled. Menacingly, he put one hand in his pocket and reached with his other hand for the car handle of my door. By this time I was so infuriated that I released the lock on the car door and simultaneously released the safety catch of my pistol.

One of the other boys chose that moment to jump from the car. He grabbed his companion by the jacket, and said, "Leave her alone. C'mon, we'll get her later."

Two days later an incendiary bomb was thrown from a speeding car. It landed in our driveway a few feet from the house where it burned itself out.

In the ensuing weeks and months the families of the Negro pupils were also constantly under attack from the segregationists. Gloria's mother was forced to resign her job in the Welfare Department because of a series of unpleasantnesses which followed when her fellow employees learned that her daughter was "one of the nine."

Carlotta's father was forced to seek employment out of the state because building contractors in Little Rock refused to employ him.

The strain was too much for Terrance Roberts' family and they moved to California.

Elizabeth's mother was fired from her job at the State School for the Blind where she was a teacher.

Of the original nine pupils, only five remained in Little Rock. They were: Carlotta Walls, Jefferson Thomas, Thelma Mothershed, Elizabeth Eckford, and Melba Pattillo. Barred from school, they took correspondence courses offered to high school pupils by the University of Arkansas.

CHAPTER XII

THE APPEAL TO THE PRESIDENT

B$_Y$ THE summer of 1959 the laws under which Governor Faubus closed the schools had been declared unconstitutional and it was rumored that the Governor was threatening to convene a Special Session of the State Legislature to ram through laws to close the schools. It was another in his series of attempts to bypass the Supreme Court decision. To avoid this maneuver, the school board announced an early opening for high schools; elementary schools were scheduled to open later. The high schools were to admit students on August 12. Registration was to begin in late July and continue into early August.

When I received word of the school board's plan, I was in New York attending the Fiftieth Anniversary Convention of the NAACP. I immediately left the Convention and returned home.

Shortly after I arrived home, a bomb made of several sticks of dynamite was hurled at our house. Having failed to secure adequate protection from local authorities, I dispatched the following telegram to the United States Attorney General in Washington:

LAST NIGHT, JULY 7, 1959, AT 10:08, A BOMB HURLED FROM AN AUTOMOBILE EXPLODED IN OUR FRONT YARD. THE BOMB FELL SHORT OF ITS TARGET AND ONLY THE LAWN WAS DAMAGED FROM THE EXPLOSION WHICH ROCKED DWELLINGS FOR SEVERAL BLOCKS. AS ADVISER TO THE LITIGANTS IN THE LITTLE ROCK SCHOOL CASE, MY HOME HAS BEEN UNDER CONSTANT ATTACK SINCE AUGUST 1957 BY LAWLESS ELEMENTS OF THIS STATE, AND MANY THREATS HAVE BEEN MADE UPON MY LIFE AND THE LIVES OF MY IMMEDIATE FAMILY. INCENDIARY BOMBS HAVE BEEN THROWN AT OUR HOME FROM AUTOMOBILES. THREE KKK CROSSES HAVE BEEN BURNED ON OUR LAWN. FIRE HAS BEEN SET TO THE HOUSE ON TWO OCCASIONS. ALL THE GLASS IN THE FRONT OF THE HOUSE HAS BEEN BROKEN OUT AND STEEL SCREENS HAD TO BE MADE TO COVER THE FRONT WINDOWS TO PROTECT OUR HOME. TO THIS DATE, NO ONE HAS BEEN APPREHENDED BY THE LAW ENFORCEMENT OFFICERS OF THIS CITY OR STATE. WE HAVE APPEALED TO THE CITY AND COUNTY FOR PROTECTION, YET THESE ATTACKS ON US AND OUR HOME CONTINUE. WE HAVE BEEN COMPELLED TO EMPLOY PRIVATE GUARDS. NOW AS A LAST RESORT, WE ARE APPEALING TO YOU TO GIVE US PROTECTION IN LITTLE ROCK, UNITED STATES OF AMERICA.

My telegram drew the following response two days later from Assistant Attorney General W. Wilson White:

THE ATTORNEY GENERAL AND I HAVE READ THE DISTRESSING ACCOUNT IN YOUR TELEGRAM OF JULY 8, 1959, OF THE HARASSMENT WHICH YOU HAVE SUFFERED SINCE THE INSTITUTION OF THE LITTLE ROCK SCHOOL DESEGREGATION CASE, CULMINATING IN THE EXPLOSION OF A BOMB ON JULY 7. AFTER CAREFUL CONSIDERATION, HOWEVER, WE ARE FORCED TO CONCLUDE THAT THERE IS NO

BASIS FOR FEDERAL JURISDICTION. ANY INVESTIGATION AND PROSECUTION OF PERSONS RESPONSIBLE FOR THE INCIDENTS WHICH YOU DESCRIBED IN YOUR TELEGRAM WOULD BE WITHIN THE EXCLUSIVE JURISDICTION OF STATE AND LOCAL AUTHORITIES. INABILITY OR FAILURE ON THE PART OF SUCH AUTHORITIES TO TAKE EFFECTIVE ACTION DOES NOT AUTHORIZE THE FEDERAL GOVERNMENT TO INTERVENE. THIS DEPARTMENT CAN TAKE ACTION ONLY WHEN THERE HAS BEEN A VIOLATION OF FEDERAL LAW. THE INFORMATION WHICH YOU FURNISH IN YOUR TELEGRAM FAILS TO DISCLOSE ANY SUCH VIOLATION.

Jefferson and Carlotta were assigned by the school board to Central High School. Three Negro girls were admitted to the newly constructed Hall High School, located in Pulaski Heights, a well-to-do section of town.

Carlotta was among the children who had gone to another city during the vacation months to attend summer school. She was in the midst of final exams at a summer school in Chicago. She could not be present, therefore, for the opening of school in Little Rock. This left Jefferson Thomas to go it alone.

Little Rock's Chief of Police, Gene Smith, announced prior to the opening that his men were prepared to deal with any eventuality.

Anyone driving through the quiet residential section of our town the morning of August 12 would have been impressed by the great profusion of roses. Little Rock is known as the "City of Roses." It was a hot and humid day. The temperature was near 90 degrees. It was a typical day in summer. The only thing that made this day different was the unusual number of cars descending on the city from West Memphis, approximately 140 miles away, and from other points throughout the State.

Little Rock's police station was the scene of considerable activity. Scores of grim-faced policemen reported to Police Chief Smith for final instructions.

Fire Chief Gann Nalley sat nervously in his office elsewhere, waiting for a call he hoped would not come.

Scores of out-of-town reporters were on the scene.

Shortly after 9 A.M., over a thousand segregationists—men, women and children—gathered on the steps of the State Capitol to protest the integration of both Central and Hall high schools. Women and children carried signs. "ARKANSAS IS FOR FAUBUS," one such sign proclaimed. "RACE MIXING IS COMMUNISTIC," shouted another sign. "GOVERNOR FAUBUS, SAVE OUR CHRISTIAN AMERICA," pleaded another.

The crowd listened to several fiery speeches. After that was heard the rhythmic chant: "We want Faubus! We want Faubus!"

The Governor made a gracious response. He appeared and spoke briefly to the crowd. After his speech, several hundred headed for Central High School, carrying Confederate flags and singing "Dixie."

At approximately 11:30 A.M., I was sitting in Jefferson Thomas' living-room with Jefferson, Minnijean and Elizabeth. A report came over the radio that the segregationists were defying the order of Police Chief Smith to disperse and that he had ordered a fire hose turned on them.

In a half hour Jefferson was scheduled to report at Central. "I know I'll catch it today," he said nervously.

Elizabeth, sitting quietly beside Jeff, turned toward him. "I'll go with you," she said.

I looked at her, startled. "Oh, Liz, no!" I cried.

"It's all right, Mrs. Bates," she said, reassuringly. "I have to go to see about having my credits transferred to Knox College anyway. So I'll go today." She added, "Besides, I just can't let Jeff go out there alone."

At 11:35 A.M. Jeff's father took the car out of the garage. From the front porch we watched as Elizabeth and Jefferson, accompanied by Carl Rowan, reporter for the *Minneapolis Tribune* and now Deputy Assistant Secretary of State, got into the car and drove off.

On returning to the living-room we heard a report coming over the radio. The police were battling the mob of several hundred, said the report, and twenty-four had thus far been arrested.

Hearing the news Jeff's mother became apprehensive. She ran from the room, sobbing pitifully. No one tried to comfort her. No one knew what to say. There were no words. Jeff's father returned with Carl Rowan in about a half hour. They reported that Elizabeth and Jefferson had entered the school —unharmed.

What happened once the children were inside was another story. As it turned out, Jeff was right when he said he was "going to catch it." No sooner had he set foot inside the school entrance than a gang of boys attacked him.

That evening, our home was buzzing with reporters. L. C. and Carl Rowan had missed their dinner because they worked late at the *State Press* office. In the kitchen, L. C. was now broiling steaks and Carl was making a salad.

Ted Poston of the *New York Post* was pecking out a story in the front bedroom. A veteran since 1957 of the "Battle of Little Rock," Ted had laid claim to the bedroom. He called it "Ted's Post." He virtually set up shop there and usually worked far into the night. When he got tired, he would push the mounds of copy paper and carbons to the floor and go to bed. Ted's routine was interrupted one night when a huge rock came crashing through the bedroom window shortly after he retired. The missile landed on his bed. After that he used the room only for working, and slept on a couch in the recreation room downstairs.

Isaac Mullen, a Deputy Sheriff, was one of our volunteer guards. He entered the kitchen while L. C. was still busy preparing the steaks. He reported that a 1959 Chevrolet had circled the block several times. He said the car had a license plate of another state but he had been unable to make it out. Two men, dressed in sport shirts with collars open at the neck, were in the car.

L. C. and some of the reporters went outside with Mr. Mullen and watched the car drive slowly past the house. They tried to catch the license plate number so that they could report it to the police. Jeff's father pulled up to our house just as the mystery car circled in front for about the twentieth time. Mr. Mullen got in Mr. Thomas' car and both followed the other car. When they drew close they observed it had a Georgia license plate.

Dr. Garman P. Freeman, our next-door neighbor, drove into his driveway just as Mr. Thomas was leaving our home at approximately 11 P.M. The car that had been circling the block now proceeded to follow Mr. Thomas' car. Mr. Mullen said to Dr. Freeman, "I don't like the looks of that car. Let's follow Thomas."

Two other volunteer guards going off duty gave Mr. Mullen their rifle and pistol. The weapons were put in the car. Around 5 A.M., Mrs. Thomas phoned my home and asked to speak to her husband. L. C. told her that Mr. Thomas had left some hours before—at about eleven o'clock. It was the first any of us knew that the men were missing. L. C. had confirmed this after checking with Mrs. Freeman and Mrs. Mullen.

I called the city and county police to inquire whether the men had met with an accident or with some other kind of trouble. The police denied knowledge of their whereabouts. I then asked the police to institute a search for the missing men.

Meanwhile, news reporters joined L. C. and me and other friends in a searching party. We covered every street in town looking for a sign of the men and their cars.

At around 8 A.M., Mrs. Mullen received a call from a prisoner who had just been released from an overnight sentence. He told her that Mr. Mullen was being held in the county jail and had asked that he notify her.

Less than twenty minutes later, officers at the county jail admitted that the three men were incarcerated there for the night but that the prisoners had since been removed to an unknown destination. They had been taken away by the State Police, we were told. We thereupon contacted the State Police who disclaimed any knowledge of the men.

Later that morning, our attorney, the late J. R. Booker, contacted the State Police who then informed him they were holding the men "for investigation."

Jefferson called me at home at around eleven thirty that morning. "I have to leave for school now," he told me. "You'll keep trying to get Dad out of jail, won't you?"

By this time word about the arrests spread throughout Little Rock. I was certain the segregationist gang at Central High School knew about it, too. Jeff's having to face the mob at school as well as the anxiety over his father's fate in the hands of hostile police seemed to me too great a strain for the boy to bear. I tried to persuade him to stay home that day.

"No," he declared. "I'm going. Dad would want me to."

When the gang met Jefferson in school, one of them blurted out, "What are you doing here? Do we have to break your head open to keep you out?"

Later that afternoon the three men were finally released from jail. Dr. Freeman and Mr. Thomas were charged with "carrying concealed weapons." Each had to put up a bail bond of $200. No charges were brought against Mr. Mullen because of his Deputy Sheriff status.

Mr. Mullen gave the following account:

"Six blocks from your house, we came upon the two cars parked at a curb. Mr. Thomas was standing with his hands raised over his head. The two men in sport shirts were searching him.

"Dr. Freeman parked near by and stayed with the car while I went over to investigate what was happening. I was wearing my holster with a .45 automatic pistol. The men identified themselves as State Police. I had my doubts since the car was unmarked and carried a Georgia plate.

"I was asked to identify myself. I showed my Pulaski County Deputy Sheriff credentials, and one of them remarked, 'Those don't mean a damn thing to us.'

"They ordered me to remove my gun. Then they went over to Dr. Freeman's car, searched it and found the pistol and rifle. They also found a second pistol in Mr. Thomas' car. The three of us were placed under arrest and taken to the State Police headquarters. They had our cars towed away.

"At State Police headquarters I heard one of the arresting officers remark to another policeman: 'We made a good haul tonight. We got all of Daisy Bates' guards.'

"We were questioned separately for over an hour and not

168

allowed to phone our families. Then we were locked up in the Pulaski County jail."

On hearing their story I sent the following telegram to President Eisenhower:

> DEAR MR. PRESIDENT, DESPITE REPEATED BOMBINGS, AT-TACKS BY GUNFIRE AND ROCKS, AND OTHER ASSAULTS ON OUR HOME—ATTACKS PROVOKED BY THE FACT THAT WE HAVE STOOD STEADFAST FOR THIS COMMUNITY'S COMPLI-ANCE WITH THE FEDERAL LAW—BOTH LOCAL AND FED-ERAL AUTHORITIES HAVE DECLINED TO PROVIDE THE MINIMUM PHYSICAL PROTECTION THAT WE HAVE RE-QUESTED. NOW STATE POLICE HAVE BEGUN TO ARREST AND HARASS THE UPSTANDING CITIZENS WHO HAVE PRO-VIDED US WITH VOLUNTEER PROTECTION, LEAVING US DEFENSELESS BEFORE THOSE WHO CONSTANTLY THREATEN OUR LIVES. I APPEAL TO YOU, MR. PRESIDENT, TO PROVIDE THE BASIC PROTECTION THAT WILL GIVE US THE FREE-DOM FROM FEAR TO WHICH CITIZENS OF OUR FREE AMERICAN SOCIETY ARE ENTITLED.

Four days after my telegram to President Eisenhower, I received the following wired message from Gerald D. Morgan, Deputy Assistant to the President:

> YOUR TELEGRAM OF AUGUST THIRTEENTH TO THE PRES-IDENT IS ACKNOWLEDGED. ALTHOUGH MATTER SEEMS TO BE ONE WITHIN THE EXCLUSIVE JURISDICTION OF LOCAL AUTHORITIES THE PRESIDENT HAS REFERRED YOUR TEL-EGRAM TO THE DEPARTMENT OF JUSTICE FROM WHICH I AM SURE IT WILL RECEIVE PROMPT AND APPROPRIATE CONSIDERATION.

Whatever was meant by "prompt and appropriate con-sideration" was never made clear beyond the mere words in the telegram. No action was forthcoming from Washington.

However, action of another kind was taking place in Little Rock. Ellis Thomas, who had been employed over ten years by International Harvester, was fired.

CHAPTER XIII

DEATH OF THE STATE PRESS

It was three o'clock in the afternoon of October 29, 1959. I stood looking out of the *State Press* window watching our accountant drive off in his car. He had just handed me a large brown envelope containing a financial statement of our business. I knew this would be his last visit to the *State Press* office. I knew without checking what the figures would reveal. My thoughts went back to an afternoon in the early fall of 1957, when a woman, not known to me before, came to our house.

She was a middle-aged white woman. She told me that she

represented a group of "Southern Christian women" who had delegated her to appeal to me "as a Southern woman." They wanted to know if I would use my influence to get Negro children to withdraw their applications to Central High School. "This would give us time to prepare the community for integration," she explained. "We need time."

"How much time?" I asked her. She couldn't say. That would be determined later. If I agreed to her plan now, we could start working together.

Next, she recommended that I call a press conference and announce that "for the good of the community" I was withdrawing my support from the students and was going to advise them to return to the Negro schools. My visitor kindly cautioned that I would no doubt be criticized in the North for this decision. But I was not to worry because the "Southern Christian women" would stand by me.

After talking to her for an hour, I was convinced that my gentle visitor was not just another one of those crackpots who were forever attempting to bring pressure on us one way or another. Finally I asked the question: "You told me what would happen if I withdrew my support from the students. What would happen if I didn't?"

She looked me straight in the eye. "You'll be destroyed—you, your newspaper, your reputation." Looking around the living-room, she added, "Everything!"

Before my visitor left, she gave me her telephone number. "You have until nine o'clock tomorrow morning to give us your answer."

Around 9 P.M. that same day Elizabeth's French tutor dropped her off at my home. Elizabeth and Jonnie, our housekeeper, watched television; and, when it got to be around eleven thirty, Elizabeth came into my bedroom and asked me if she could stay over. I said, "Of course." She phoned her mother and told her she was spending the night with us.

I was still awake around 2 A.M. trying to formulate my answer to the woman visitor when I heard a muffled cry coming from Elizabeth's bedroom. When I went to investigate I found Elizabeth tossing restlessly on the bed. I knew she must have been reliving the frightful experience of the shrieking, howling mob in front of Central High School. The compassion I felt for her only deepened the anger I bore against her persecutors.

Elizabeth finally quieted down and I walked into my living-room and looked out into the dark street through the large picture window. The glass was now held together by masking tape.

How proud my husband and I had been two years before when we moved into this newly constructed house. For L. C. and me, it was the fulfillment of years of planning and saving. When the house was finally built, over five hundred of our friends came to wish us well. I recalled the words of our minister, Rev. Rufus K. Young, as he prayed for us. ". . . God bless this home and may peace and happiness forever dwell within it."

Jonnie entered the room, still looking half asleep. "Did I hear a scream?" she inquired anxiously.

"Yes, you heard Elizabeth," I said.

The bright glare of headlights suddenly flooded the room. We looked out and saw a car crammed with teen-agers. They cruised slowly past the house.

Our house guard, Otis Robertson, who took up a position in the carport, raised his gun in readiness. Just as the car reached the end of our property line, a huge firecracker exploded in the street.

Little Rock Nine and friends at NAACP's 49th annual convention in Cleveland, left to right, standing: Terrance Roberts, Thelma Mothershed, Gloria Ray, Jefferson Thomas, Kivie Kaplan, Minnijean Brown, Ernest Green, Mrs. L. C. Bates, Dr. James E. Levy; seated: Carlotta Walls, Melba Patillo and Elizabeth Eckford. Mr. Kaplan of Boston is co-chairman of the NAACP life membership committee. Dr. Levy is president of the Association's Cleveland branch. *State Historical Society of Wisconsin, Daisy Bates Collection.*

Daisy Bates. *Special Collections Department, David W. Mullins Library, University of Arkansas.*

L. C. Bates. *State Historical Society of Wisconsin, Daisy Bates Collection.*

Paratroopers, ordered to Little Rock by President Eisenhower in September 1957, escort nine Negro students into the large high school. Earlier, Governor Orval E. Faubus had directed National Guardsmen to surround the building to prevent these students from entering. *UPI/Bettmann Newsphotos.*

National Guardsmen, fully armed, stand watch in front of Central High School. *UPI/Bettmann Newsphotos.*

Governor Orval E. Faubus delivers his radio and television address to the nation, during which he bitterly attacked the action of the Federal government in sending troops to "occupy" Little Rock and enforce school integration. *UPI/Bettmann Newsphotos.*

Wiley Branton and Thurgood Marshall, NAACP case attorneys. *State Historical Society of Wisconsin, Daisy Bates Collection. Earl Davy, photographer.*

Virgil T. Blossom. Superintendent of Schools. *UPI/Bettmann Newsphotos.*

Mob marches on Central High School to keep Negro students from entering. *Arkansas Gazette.*

With bayonets fixed, soldiers of the 101st Airborne Division march away a group of angry men. *UPI/Bettmann Newsphotos.*

Ellis Thomas, left, father of Jefferson Thomas, is taken from State Police head-quarters by Sgt. C. C. Clayton. Thomas would be charged with carrying concealed weapons. *UPI/Bettmann Newsphotos.*

Local police stand ready to halt marchers in front of school. *Arkansas Gazette.*

Jefferson Thomas stands alone, as white students noisily harass him as he waits for transportation home. *UPI/Bettmann Newsphotos.*

Shaken, Jonnie sat down on the couch, staring blankly out of the window. I began to pace nervously around the room, pausing to look at the stack of foreign newspapers piled high on the dining-room table. As I thumbed through them, the large black headlines read pretty much the same in all languages: 15-YEAR-OLD GIRL MOBBED IN LITTLE ROCK. Many of them carried pictures of Elizabeth Eckford surrounded by the jeering mob, and photos of the bayonet-carrying Arkansas national guardsmen who barred her entrance to Central High School.

Jonnie broke the silence. "Mrs. Bates, how are you going to answer that woman in the morning?"

"I have no idea," I said.

Jonnie sat silently for several minutes. Finally she gave a deep sigh and got up from the couch. "I'm going to bed," she said. "The reporters will be coming in early in the morning. I know you will make the right decision. God will show you the way."

Alone, I walked around the living-room and paused in front of the table that held a small white china vase. I picked it up. Idly I ran my finger over the dark jagged line where it had been mended years before. I remembered how proud I had been when the vase had been given to me on my fifth birthday by my adopted grandmother. It had been her mother's before her. This fragile vase was my most prized possession. It could have been smuggled from the "big house" during slavery days, or bought with money earned by blood and sweat from the heaped-up junk cart of a traveling peddler. Somehow, to me it represented my roots, my family, their appreciation for beauty at a time when they, too, were subjected to brutality and degradation.

To this day I have not been able to answer to my own

173

satisfaction why I suddenly hurled the vase against the brick fireplace, shattering it into a thousand tiny pieces. Maybe it was the realization that after all of these years, in the minds of the white Southerners, the roots of the Negro were shallow indeed, regardless of his accomplishments or how hard he worked, and that his roots could be torn up at their slightest whim.

Dawn was breaking. In five more hours I had to call my lady visitor with my decision. I went outside and took the guard's gun. "You can go now," I told him. "It will be daylight soon. I can't sleep so I'll sit in the car for a while."

I rested the .45 automatic pistol in my lap while Skippy, our cocker spaniel, went to sleep on the seat beside me. I began asking myself questions. Do I have the guts to tell the bigots to go to hell? Do I have the right to destroy sixteen years of my husband's life's work?

The slow drizzling rain had turned into a heavy shower. I was frustrated and angry and the weather matched my mood. The thought occurred to me that maybe I should take a vacation. Just leave Little Rock for a while. Maybe the problem would just go away. Or maybe someone else would assume the responsibility of getting the students into Central. I tried to reason that, after all, it was the responsibility of the Federal Government to protect the rights of the students. Yet I knew, from bitter experience, that the Federal authorities had shown little interest in protecting the rights of Negroes.

I looked out of the car and my eyes fell on the closed window of the bedroom where Elizabeth lay in restless sleep. I thought about this tragic youngster who, at age fifteen, had shown more courage than I could possibly muster at this moment.

I began to think that in the struggle for freedom there could be no turning back, no strategic withdrawals, subterfuges, or compromises. What I was going to tell my "Southern Christian" friend was now perfectly clear.

Promptly at 9 A.M. I telephoned her as we had agreed and informed her that I had arrived at an answer to her plea. My answer, I told her, was "No!" I made sure to add that I was truly sorry for her and all of her ilk—bigots parading behind the standard of "Christianity."

L. C. had not known about the visit of the Southern gentlewoman. Now I was eager to report the incident and to tell him about my decision. It was as though the entire episode involved me personally and the decision was mine alone to make. Yet this was obviously not the case. At stake was the life of the *State Press*. L. C. had to know. I hastened to the *State Press* office.

When I finished the story, L. C. rose from his desk, walked to the window and gazed reflectively at the outdoors. I simply watched him and said nothing. The only sounds that were heard came from the presses that were turning out a fresh edition of our newspaper. At that moment I wondered for how long the machines would continue to do their work for us. I was sure that the same thoughts were now going through L. C.'s mind.

Finally he turned, gripping the chair back so that the veins in his hands stood out prominently, and looked down at me with a tired, defeated expression on his face. I tried to say it was the only decision I could make. But he waved his hand to silence me. "No, Daisy, you did the right thing."

He said nothing more. He simply went back to his desk and shuffled a few papers he had been working on when I came to talk with him. I made no effort to discuss the matter further, because when he sat down at his desk I saw tears in his eyes.

In a matter of a few weeks we watched sixteen years of our lives being quickly chopped away, as we received curt, polite—and some not polite—notes from business firms and advertising agencies canceling their advertising contracts. Some contracts were not renewed as they expired. The advertisements of some of our largest and most substantial clients disappeared from the pages of the *State Press*. Among them were Southwestern Bell Telephone Company, Arkansas-Louisiana Gas Company, Arkansas Power and Light Company, real estate housing developments, and many of the off-Main Street merchants.

One of our long-time advertisers, a grocer, whose place of business stayed open until midnight, received an anonymous telephone call, warning that if he ran one more advertisement in our paper his store would be bombed. On the night of the anonymous phone call, three tough-looking men stalked into the grocery store and surveyed the shelves of groceries. On the way out, they turned and cast one long, menacing stare at the proprietor and his wife. The next day the wife related the frightening experience to a friend. "Don't you think they are bluffing?" the friend said.

"Maybe so," said the wife, "but we can't afford to take the chance."

The segregationists scored another successful intimidation and the grocer stopped advertising in the *State Press*.

During the period that we fought for our economic survival, and indeed, at times, for our very lives, I often felt a deep resentment and bitterness toward those who were using the lives of children as pawns in a political game. But as people throughout the world heard of our plight through the mass media, hundreds of letters of encouragement poured into the *State Press* office. Many contained checks of a dollar to one hundred dollars.

One of the most touching letters came from a ten-year-old boy who lived near McComb, Mississippi. A fifty-cent piece was pasted to a crumpled cardboard. The message was printed on lined notebook paper. It read: "Dear Miss Daisy, I am ten years old and this is all I have. I was saving it to buy Mom a Christmas present. I want you to have it. I know she won't mind. I want to help." The letter was signed, "Larry."

L. C. and I were grateful to all the wonderful people and organizations who were concerned about our welfare. But what shook me to the very depths was the stark realization that in this allegedly free and enlightened society only a small minority concerned itself about the cruelties and injustices that were being perpetrated against Negro children.

We used all the resources at our command to save the paper. However, it soon became apparent that we were fighting a losing battle. I gave L. C. the report of our assets and liabilities. Its meaning was all too clear.

Robert Scott, our linotype operator, had been with us over ten years. He was cleaning his machine when I handed him his weekly paycheck and two weeks' severance pay. He just sat there looking at it. No words were necessary. Everyone on the staff was aware of the financial condition of the paper. Everyone knew that no paper can exist without advertisers.

Peter Campbell had been with the *State Press* family six years, ever since he was out of high school. He was distributing type when his last check was handed to him. He turned it back to me. "You only owe me for one week." he said.

The office manager, Mrs. Thressa Jones, a short, plump, cheerful person, quick to laugh, easy to cry, remained loyal to the end. When we were forced to reduce the office staff, she quickly agreed to assume the responsibilities of two secretaries in addition to her own duties. Now she looked at her check and started to cry.

The door was closed on the *State Press* and on eighteen years of our lives. No last good-bys, no final editorials. The break had to be clean and sharp, for the pain was too deep.

At exactly 5 P.M., the *State Press* had breathed its last word.

CHAPTER XIV

WHITE CASUALTIES

THE STRUGGLE of the American Negro does not lack for martyrs, and the so-called "Little Rock Nine" will surely be counted among them. But the Negro was often not alone in his struggle. Many white fellow-Americans joined ranks with him. And they have paid the price.

I offer their stories in the hope that whites and Negroes in other Southern communities, where the battle is yet to come, may be encouraged to stand firm but with full knowledge of what to expect.

Heroism is not something that can be weighed, measured,

or compared, but I do know that these white Americans, each in his own way, should be considered heroic. If their efforts seemed to them in vain, or ineffective, they possibly deserve all the more honor for continuing, for not *betraying*, their aid to democracy. Some did break, or were broken, but none betrayed.

At the height of the Little Rock crisis, few white citizens came forward in support of law and order. Not one labor leader, for example, spoke out. Initially, several ministers voiced their approval of a peaceful fulfillment of the school board's integration plan. But, as the battle lines were gathered, they became silent. A single exception was the Reverend Dunbar Ogden, who continued to address himself to the conscience of Little Rock, warning the citizens of the impending storm.

A few leaders in other fields also held firm. The more they withstood abuse and threats, the more their vision and determination were sharpened. They became active allies of the Negro citizens fighting for human decency. Inevitably they soon became casualties of vindictive hate attacks. Until this time most had taken their freedom for granted. After all, they were members of the "privileged class" that perpetuated the political and social enslavement of millions of Negroes. They had no reason to doubt their constitutional freedom. But now the same vicious system that deprived Negroes of their rights turned on them.

Harry Ashmore, the liberal editor of the *Arkansas Gazette,* wrote his own epitaph in Little Rock when he printed his first editorial criticizing Governor Faubus for calling out the troops. In 1958 he won a Pulitzer prize for his constructive editorials during the Little Rock crisis. The Ashmore family was constantly subjected to intense pressure from the segregationists until, finally, he resigned his position and moved his family to California.

Mayor Woodrow Mann, who bitterly condemned Faubus for the invasion of Little Rock, had wired President Eisenhower asking for troops. He, too, later left the hate-ridden city, where he was born, because of pressure from segregationists.

Virgil T. Blossom, Superintendent of the Little Rock School District, was voted "Man of the Year" in 1955 by the citizens of Little Rock, ironically, for his plan of gradual integration.

After Faubus closed the high schools in 1958, all but one of the six-member school board resigned. Only Dr. Dale Alford remained on the board. Shortly thereafter a city election was held to replace the school board members. When the newly elected board members took office they evidently did not feel as amenable toward the integration plan as the former members. For almost their first official act was to fire Superintendent Virgil Blossom.

Mr. Blossom later accepted a position as Superintendent of Schools in San Antonio, Texas.

All of these white Southerners came face to face with the agonizing fact that the same system they had supported all these years—the same system that had been used to deny Negroes their rights—was now being used against them. Those who dared speak up became pariahs. They were fired from their jobs, put out of business, ostracized by their friends, driven from town. And three met with death.

The morning of March 19, 1960, had been a routine one for our household. Jonnie had served breakfast, and everyone was about to begin the day when the flash came over the radio: "Little Rock Chief of Police Eugene G. Smith has killed his wife and taken his own life!" We stood stunned as we listened to the sparse details: "Smith pumped three fatal bullets into his wife as she sat at the kitchen table, then turned the pistol on himself and fired a bullet into his head." I retched. Jonnie rushed to my side and helped me to my bedroom. "I'll call Dr. Woods," she said.

"No, Jonnie, I'll be all right."

"But you're cold as ice, Mrs. Bates."

Jonnie must have fussed over me for some time. Then she undressed me and put me to bed. I remember thinking as I lay there, "This must be a nightmare, it *must* be—but soon I'll awaken." Indeed, the previous three years had been a nightmare. A hollow feeling of loneliness and fear gripped me as I lay in the quiet room thinking, "Smith is dead. Maybe we'll be next."

The description in the press, of the body of Mary Smith lying across a chair while Gene Smith was sprawled in a pool of blood at her feet, should have shocked the silent citizens of Little Rock into action. It didn't.

Later I stood watching the funeral procession. Some people were weeping openly on the streets. I thought, "Weep, my city. Maybe tears will wash away your shame."

After the double funeral, the silent citizens who had wept became even more silent while the merchants of hate became even more vocal.

Gene Smith, forty-seven years old, was a big, handsome six-foot, two hundred pounder. He had come up through the ranks during twenty-four years of service. When Governor Faubus was forced by the Federal Court to withdraw the Arkansas national guardsmen and to stop interfering with integration at Central High, Smith was Assistant Chief of Police. When school authorities wondered how they could protect the Negro students, Smith came to their aid. "Just give me the men and I will protect the children," he said.

When I was told to have the students assemble at my house by 8:15 A.M. on September 23, I asked who would protect the students. The reply was: "Smith, of course."

At 6 A.M. the next morning, facing a mob of one thousand, Smith stood with one hundred of the department's best men, blockading the streets to Central—a school he and his children had attended. Later, when the mob learned that the Negro students had gone inside the school, it surged against the police lines, ignoring Gene Smith's command to halt. One of the mob's leaders ran up to Smith, and Smith knocked him to the pavement. Many were arrested and sent to jail.

Benjamin Fine of *The New York Times* told me that Smith was like a one-man army. But when reporters questioned Smith on how he stood on the issue of integration, he replied, "That's out of my province. Our function is to do everything we can to protect life and property and preserve the public peace. And that's what we do every day."

Although Smith's actions drew expressions of appreciation from local businessmen and city officials, from that day on he became a prime target of the segregationists. They accused him of brutality in protecting the Negro students. They hurled such epithets at him as "Gestapo!" "Yellow dog!" "Nigger-loving red!" and "Judas!"

Chief of Police Marvin H. Potts resigned in October, 1957. In January, 1958, over the strong objection of the Central High School Mothers League, Smith was promoted to replace him.

The tense and weary city breathed relief as the curtain was

drawn on the 1957-58 school year. Little Rock was beginning to relax; but there was no chance of relaxation for Gene Smith. Governor Faubus closed the schools for the next academic year, and Smith was faced with hundreds of white teen-agers driving wildly through the streets, almost daily, shouting their approval of Governor Faubus' action.

Ironically, the first blood to flow in the streets (as Faubus had predicted) was the blood of a white man, spilled by riotous white teen-agers. He was sixty-seven-year-old R. L. McGoodwin, struck at a street crossing by a car in a caravan of some two hundred students. Several days later he died of multiple injuries in a Little Rock hospital. Mr. McGoodwin, according to witnesses of the fatal accident, had just finished waving his approval to the very students who struck him down.

A few days prior to the opening of the high schools on August 12, I talked with Police Chief Smith. "Do you think we'll have trouble?" I asked.

"I hope not," he replied. "However, from all indications, we are going to catch hell from the segregationists. But we'll be ready for them. And I also have a plan to keep the reporters in line."

On the eve of the high schools' opening, August 11, Smith's fears were realized. Four shots were fired from a passing car at my husband and a group of reporters. They included Ted Poston, of the *New York Post*, and Carl Rowan, then with the *Minneapolis Tribune*. One of the shots entered the home of a neighboring white family, narrowly missing one of the children and embedding itself in a living-room wall.

The next day the name of Eugene Smith was again heard

throughout the world. The front pages of the world press, news magazines, and television and movie screens all flashed the picture of a big, well-tailored figure in a pork-pie straw hat standing in front of uniformed police facing an angry mob.

Smith had faced mobs in Little Rock before. Conflict had made him famous—a hero to some, a symbol of sturdy, law-abiding, middle-of-the-road democracy to others, and a villain, an object of hatred, a turncoat to the white supremacists.

On this morning, a caravan of segregrationists' cars drove into Little Rock. After a speech by Governor Faubus in front of the State Capitol building, the crowd flowed into the streets of the city—shouting, singing, urging all bystanders to join in with them. The crowd surged toward the grounds of Central High School to prevent one lone Negro boy from entering the premises.

The police and fire departments formed a solid line across the mob's path. Chief of Police Smith used a megaphone to make sure that everyone heard him. *"We want no trouble,"* he called. *"Break it up! Go home!"*

One news reporter gave this account of the scene:

"The crowd surged forward but the police pushed them back. At Smith's direction, fire hoses were turned on the crowds, drenching them with water. Nightsticks were brought into play. Some men were taken from the scene with blood trickling down the sides or backs of their heads. By the end of the day, twenty-four had been arrested, some of them women, charged with either loitering or disturbing the peace. In one or two instances the charge was lodged of assaulting an officer."

After the events of that day, Smith again caught the full

impact of the vicious attacks of the segregationists. He also was on the receiving end of countless court suits filed against him because of the arrests he had ordered. Twenty-odd persons who were arrested later filed damage suits against Smith. The damages sought aggregated almost $500,000. The charge: Smith had violated their civil rights!

A Little Rock newspaper quoted one of the lawyers for the plaintiffs as saying: ".... To begin with, I want to make clear that the suits against Chief Smith have nothing to do with integration or segregation. The suits involve a violation of rights."

It was less than a month after the police and fire departments had used their combined forces to disperse the mobs that a new bombardment of headlines again exploded in the Little Rock press.

Some time during the evening of September 7 (Labor Day), three separate but obviously connected bombings had literally rocked Little Rock. A city-owned station wagon used by Fire Chief Gann Nalley—parked in front of his house—was bombed. Chief Nalley had been one of the main participants in dispersing the August 12 mob by using fire hoses. The School Board Administration building was bombed. And the business office of Little Rock's Mayor was almost completely destroyed by a bomb.

After a thorough police investigation, five men were finally indicted and brought to trial. Of these, three emerged as principals in the affair, and around one of them, in particular, heated passions and deep-rooted prejudices began to emerge. The three men included two truck drivers, J. D. Sims and Jesse Raymond Perry. The third was an ardent, outspoken segregationist, E. A. Lauderdale, Sr., owner of the

Lauderdale Roofing and Building Materials Company. During his flamboyantly reported trial, it was hinted clearly that Mr. Lauderdale was high in the councils of the Ku Klux Klan. He was referred to as the "mastermind" of the bombing plot. Indeed, since so many of Little Rock's buildings were topped with his products, he had literally blown off his own roofs!

At the trial, evidence of a cache of dynamite, secreted most theatrically in a dried-up creek bed near a deserted house, was produced. There were charges by Lauderdale's lawyers that Smith was having them "tailed" and their telephones tapped. Smith denied these charges. The defense also claimed that the men could not receive a fair trial because of the highly charged emotional atmosphere, but a change of venue was denied.

The men were found guilty by the jury in the Arkansas Circuit Court, and the jury recommended that Lauderdale receive a sentence of three years' imprisonment, plus a fine of $500.

Constant harassment and daily threats of violence were serious strains on even so solid a man as Gene Smith. Persecutions never lagged. The days stretched into weeks, the weeks into months, until finally seven months elapsed. On Friday, March 18, 1960, his twenty-year-old son, Raymond Eugene Smith, who was married and a father, and was attending Harding College, pleaded guilty with three other students to a series of thefts in Searcy, Arkansas. Young Smith was fined $250 and given a three-years' suspended sentence. The others received $250 fines and five-years' suspended sentences.

Eugene Smith was a man of great personal courage. He was born and reared in Little Rock. He became a football and track star at the high school now known as Central. A graduate of the F.B.I. Academy, he had served as instructor at the University of Arkansas Police Academy. Later he served in the United States Navy. Smith was obviously a man trained to withstand much more than the ordinary pressures of life. But who can possibly term as "ordinary pressure" the grinding horror that had settled on Little Rock?

Smith had become the hub of a wheel that couldn't, or wouldn't, stop turning. Perhaps his son's conviction had finally shattered the spirit of this able police officer who had already suffered so much at the hands of the segregationists. For on the day of that conviction, Smith killed his wife and then himself.

The following morning, March 19, at ten o'clock, a neighbor entered the Smith home and discovered the bodies. A pistol lay near by. When the police arrived, it was determined that the double tragedy had occurred at about nine thirty the previous evening. Later, the county coroner, Dr. Howard A. Dishongh, established that Chief Smith had fired three fatal shots into his wife as she sat at the kitchen table, then turned the pistol on himself and fired the bullet into his head.

And so, with a tragedy that was officially labeled murder-suicide, the star-crossed career of Eugene Granville Smith was ended. Whatever else that was to happen in Little Rock, Gene Smith would not be a part of it. He remains only in the memory of those who were part of those fateful happenings in Little Rock as a courageous, dedicated police officer who did his duty as he saw it, standing for law and order even when the Governor of his State did not.

The tragedy of Chief Smith is almost inextricably bound up with my own Little Rock experiences. As I lay in my bed the morning I learned of his death, I remarked to Jonnie, "This might have been my story."

"Judas betrayed Jesus Christ, Benedict Arnold betrayed a country, and you, Dunbar, have betrayed a race!"

This was the harsh judgment thrown at the Reverend Dunbar Ogden, Jr., by one of his boyhood friends. His friend was not alone in feeling that Mr. Ogden had turned traitor to the white race. For Mr. Ogden was a Southerner whose roots lay deep in the old plantation tradition; his heritage was linked to the slave-owning South. His great-grandfather, David Hunt, was said to have owned more slaves than any other man in Mississippi—and probably the South. His uncle, Fred Ogden, led an uprising against the New Orleans Metropolitan Police, which was a Negro law enforcement agency established by the Federal Government during the Reconstruction. His father held a high ministerial post in the Presbyterian Church and had served some of the largest and most distinguished congregations in the South.

Because of Mr. Ogden's background and his present eminence, his friends felt betrayed. What had he done?

The Ogden family moved to Little Rock in 1954, almost unnoticed except by the members of the Central Presbyterian Church. They arrived at a time when the South was splitting into two distinct and disturbing camps. One group was hailing the May 17, 1954, Supreme Court decision as "right and just." The other was condemning it as "Communist-inspired" and "a usurpation of the rights of all white men." Mr. Ogden was not unaccustomed to such polemics, and he and his family soon settled comfortably into the pattern of the Little Rock community.

Mr. Ogden performed the usual duties of a minister and participated, without fanfare, in the work of many civic organizations. He was chaplain for the Exceptional Children PTA and the Little Rock Chapter of the United Palsy, Inc. He was also an active member of the Civitan Club Committee for Aid to Mentally Retarded Children.

His wife, an outgoing, able woman devoted to her husband and family, was also active in community affairs. Two of their sons, Jonathan, nineteen, and Paul, an eight-year-old with an infectious smile, were both deaf. Mrs. Ogden's participation in the Association of Parent and Teacher for the Deaf was therefore especially close to her heart. She worked so assiduously that she was elected State President of the association.

The Ogdens had two older sons, David, twenty-one, who worked for the Arkansas State Highway Commission and later for the Y.M.C.A., and Dunbar III, who was studying at the University of Munich under a German government scholarship.

When I first visited the Ogden family, some three years after their arrival, I was impressed by the unity and humor of the family. They seemed so devoted to one another. But I am getting ahead of my story.

The first time Mr. Ogden attracted my attention was when he was elected President of the Greater Little Rock Interracial Interdenominational Ministerial Alliance in June, 1957. It was this that led me to telephone and ask him to walk with the students to Central High School.

When I talked to him that night, he was momentarily hesitant. "If it's God's will, I'll be there." Later he admitted that much of his hesitancy was due to simple fear. But much in his background and tradition also caused him to wonder and hesitate. "I was still thinking in terms of 'separate but equal,' " he explained. "I was incapable of a real relationship with Negro friends because I was still condescending in my attitude."

The next morning, when the children assembled to go to school, Mr. Ogden was there to walk with them. With him was his son David. The father was pleased and proud that his son had accompanied him. "When I left the house this morning," he told me, "I wasn't sure how many would be here. I phoned all the ministers that I thought might come, but there was doubt in their voices. 'Isn't this a bit dramatic?' 'Is this the responsibility of the ministry?' In fact, more than one replied, 'I'm not sure that this is the will of God.' But as I was getting into the car, David came out of the house and said, 'Dad, I'll go with you. You may need a bodyguard.' "

Only three other ministers had come, and Mr. Ogden said somewhat apologetically, "I am very discouraged that I wasn't able to get more, but frankly, I had to pray for courage myself. All I could think of was a pop bottle hitting me on the back of my head."

He never suspected that the white citizens of Little Rock would turn on him. He was, after all, a minister and a Southerner. But that day, when he saw the stored-up hate in the mob and their contorted faces, when he heard them screaming not only for the blood of the nine Negro children but for his and all connected with him, he realized how vicious was the system under which he had lived all his life. "I became aware of where segregation led. I had to make a decision," he told me later.

At first the reaction against Mr. Ogden was mild. A close friend asked, "Why did you do it, Dunbar?"

Other parishioners loyally defended him. One remarked:

"After all, he is President of that Interracial Ministerial Alliance. With a position like that, he had to do something for reasons of face. After all, you know he didn't volunteer."

Mr. Ogden still could have retained his following, his prestige. He had only to turn his back on us. Instead, he organized and moderated a state-wide meeting of interdenominational clergymen that released a religious manifesto in support of our struggle.

The hate forces did not lie idle. And so, his fellow clergymen began tempering their public remarks or became silent in full retreat. Soon he was a lone voice crying to the conscience of the people.

Mr. Ogden was not aiming to become a martyr by his actions, or to appear holier-than-thou, although he was accused of both. He had seen and was beginning to grapple with the harsh realities around him. And it was this that led his friend to write, "You, Dunbar, have betrayed a race."

To the segregationists, Mr. Ogden had become a traitor. He had deserted the cause and they were duty bound to see him pay the price. To do this, it was not necessary to don masks and white sheets or ride him out of town on a rail; all that was needed was to withhold the customary financial pledges to his church. Earlier he had been warned by a heavy contributor who complained that "the pastor's racial activities take too much time from his duties, and that's not exactly what we pay him for."

Later less subtle pressures were employed. Members of his church stopped attending services, stopped giving financial support, and finally forced him to resign. Of course, everything was done with decorum, because it was not the "roughnecks" uptown but the "moneybags" downtown—including some of Little Rock's "nicest people" and Mr. Ogden's "best friends"—who got rid of him.

The night before Mr. and Mrs. Ogden left Little Rock for his new charge as assistant minister at the First Presbyterian Church in Huntington, West Virginia, they came to see me. As we talked, I noticed a remarkable physical change in Mr. Ogden's face—deepened lines on his brow, tired and sad eyes. I was reminded of his "Calvary"—the insulting telephone calls he received night and day, the abuse and verbal indignities heaped upon his family, the rejection by his lifelong friends, and the loss of his church. This reflection of the price he had paid for decency caused me to regret having made that first telephone call to him. "I'm sorry I got you into this," I said.

He was silent for a moment. Then he said, "Don't feel sorry. If I had to do it all over again, I would. I believe that I'm a better Christian for having been privileged to participate in such a worthy cause."

After Mr. Ogden left the city, his son David fell heir to the hate attacks of the segregationists. David, as I knew him, was a personable, warm-hearted, and sensitive young man whose ideals had been strengthened by his father's role in our struggle. I became aware of David's subjection to the constant cruelty of the hate groups. I learned about it during a talk one evening with a white friend of mine. He had come by the house and asked if I knew that David was still in town.

"Yes," I replied.

"Well, Daisy," he went on, "here's something you don't know. Tonight, as I was entering the theater, I observed a group of boys harassing another youngster just beyond the ticket window. I paid no particular attention until I heard your name mentioned. Someone was saying, 'Why ain't you with Daisy Bates, nigger-lover?' I turned and saw a group of hoodlums taunting David. They surrounded him and were yelling, 'We ran your old man out of town! You should have gone with him!' It was horrible. But David stood there. He just stood there and didn't bat an eyelash."

The story unnerved me. After all, David had done no more than accompany his father the first day the children tried to enter Central. I turned to my white friend and asked, "Did it occur to you to go to David's aid?"

He sat quietly for a moment. "I just didn't have the courage," he admitted.

I called David and asked how he was getting along.

"I'm all right, Mrs. Bates," he said, "don't worry about me. How are you?"

Although David never complained, never cried out, things were far from all right. Segregationists had caused such unpleasantness on his job at the Y.M.C.A. that he was forced to leave. He took a job as bookkeeper in one of the downtown firms and established cordial relations with his fellow workers. Then one day a segregationist spotted him while at lunch and followed him back to his job. David's employer and fellow workers were soon informed of his identity. He began receiving "traitor" treatment. One of the men with whom David had developed a friendship said, "I'm ashamed to know you. If I had my way, you'd be run out of town." Another co-worker began to barrage David with vile names. David remained outwardly calm. This apparently annoyed the worker so much that he struck David with his fist. Still David did not fight back. Instead, he resigned the next day.

David went to his family in Huntington, West Virginia. He looked for a job there but was unsuccessful. Finally he decided that he would go to California to find work there. On his way he planned to visit a friend in Tennessee.

En route he stopped at a motel.

Who knows what goes on in the mind of a sensitive and gentle person? Who knows what he asks himself? What answer does he find?

On the night of June 22, 1960, David Ogden raised a shotgun to his chest and killed himself.

During the spring of 1958 I was so involved with the day-to-day problems of the children at Central and with the safety of their families and L. C. and myself that I scarcely knew what was happening to anyone else in our town.

I knew in a general way that the vast majority of citizens had not participated in the mob actions. I knew also that however shocked and ashamed they might be, they had kept silent about it.

But not until Bill Hadley, Jr., dropped over to see us one night in March, 1958, did I have any idea to what extent the outbreak of hate and cruelty had effected the perfectly decent people in our community. I had fancied that only the Capital Citizens Council, the Mothers League, the Klan people and their recruits were the hostile ones. And I had thought that only the nine children and myself were their main targets.

Bill was one of the many white persons I regarded as a good friend in Little Rock. I had known him for years. Until the summer before, when he had opened a public relations and advertising office, Bill had been probably the best-known and most popular radio and TV commentator in Arkansas. He specialized in political reporting. I had served on many committees with him. We had worked particularly closely on the Mayor's Committee, first set up by Pratt Remmel—our first Republican mayor since Reconstruction—to entertain distinguished foreign visitors from Asia, Africa, and Europe.

Bill came in the door and flung himself on our living-room couch. His smile was as warm as ever, but I noticed a certain droop in his big shoulders. I had always felt that Bill was one of the most self-assured persons I had ever known.

"Hi, Bill!" I said cordially. "How about a hot cup of tea?"

"I sure could use one," he said.

Something in his voice—a well-trained, musical voice that had been familiar to people from one end of Arkansas to the other—made me look at him more closely. His smile faded and his eyes, usually clear and candid, were red-rimmed and strained.

"Bill, are you ill?" I asked softly.

"No, Daisy." He looked at me searchingly. "What about you? You look tired. You must be catching holy hell." He said the last two words almost in awe.

"Yes, a little," I said. "But I haven't seen you in a month of Sundays. I want to hear about you and Jean and the kids."

Jean was a native Arkansan, while Bill had grown up in Massachusetts. The daughter of a prominent minister from Lonoke, Arkansas, Jean had met Bill during the war, when he was in training camp in Stuttgart, Arkansas. They were married a year later and, after the war, settled in Little Rock. Bill had been in radio before the war, and almost overnight he became a favorite radio commentator in Little Rock. Except for five years when he was with a Providence, Rhode Island, station, the Hadleys had lived in Little Rock.

"The family's all right, and I'm all right—oh, what the hell, I can't fool you, Daisy." He smiled again. Jonnie brought us the tea. Bill stirred silently for a moment. "I guess that's the reason I came out here. Thought if I could unload on you, you'd cheer me up. But I feel better already. Just being with you folks makes me feel at ease, so maybe I'll say no more."

"Oh, no, you don't, Bill Hadley. You don't get out of it that easily," I shot back. "What's up? Start talking!"

L. C. excused himself, explaining he had to join Mr. Thomas outside in guarding the house, and that he would be back later.

"Holler if you need any help!" said Bill. Then he turned to me. "Daisy, I'm discovering there's no middle ground. No middle ground at all."

"What do you mean?" I asked, knowing full well what he meant.

"I just left a meeting," he said, and wearily waving a hand, he added, "It doesn't matter what meeting. You know how many boards and committees I'm on. Listen, do people in this town talk about anything but integration these days? We're meeting supposedly on something else. But they bring it in every time. And, of course, Daisy, when they do, I can't stay out of it. I speak my mind.

"Only this evening it was different. For the first time I actually felt utterly alone. It's frightening—not for me, but for them. I told them, at one point, 'The nine Negro students at Central—no eight, now that they suspended one—they'll do all right. But what about yourselves? Are you sure you will? Don't we have a community conscience any more?' "

"Then what happened? Did anyone else speak up?" I asked.

"Oh, I'm sure some *felt* as I did," Bill said. "Most of them consider themselves 'moderates.' Yes, someone else did speak up—a very respected woman with whom I'd been friendly. And she let me have it right between the eyes. She used all the stereotypes, all the clichés. She shocked me because I

197

hadn't ever pictured her that way. The others were less extreme, arguing that it was no longer a question of integration or segregation, but State's rights!"

"Bill," I said, "I've always felt that when the chips were down on the race issue, you'd come up on the right side."

"They're down, Daisy. They're surely down," he said, draining his cup. He glanced at me quizzically. "I suppose this all seems like small potatoes to you, Daisy, compared to the problems you have to deal with." He lit a cigarette and inhaled deeply. Then he went over and pulled the curtains back to inspect our window. "I see you still have your battle scars."

"Yes," I said. "No use our getting a new window. It would just invite a fresh stone, or bottle, or something worse, hurled through it. But let's talk about your problem. You still haven't finished your story."

"This is it, Daisy," he began again. "It's hard to make it seem real, but—" He started pacing the floor, then sat down, scowling. "It's just that I've seen this same thing happen in too many of the organizations I'm affiliated with. Of course, a good third of them are interracial, but I'm talking about the all-white groups."

"I suppose all the people at your meeting were influential?" I asked.

"Oh, absolutely, all of them—doctors, professionals, well-to-do businessmen, men whose careers were pretty well made. They're the only ones who have time to give to these organizations, you know that. And it's this that burns me up. They're the very ones who always take the lead in every fund-raising and other civic activity, but they might as well be in Florida for all the good they're doing in this crisis!

"That's what I meant when I said there's no middle

ground. You have to choose sides very quickly—immediately —even if your only support is to remain silent. I've never seen a wall go up so fast in a community. And, Daisy, there's no door in that wall." His voice dropped and he shook his head. He looked baffled, and his eyes looked as though they were searching my face for an answer. "Once you're on that side, either side, you are there," he took up again. "And there isn't any way to cross over. If you do climb and cross over, you're going to be suspected by both sides."

Yes, I thought, he's finally learning what Negroes have always known and lived with—how sharply lines are drawn in a southern community. But when I spoke, I only murmured: "Poor guy, it must be very rough for you, finding out how mean and heartless your own people can be."

"And the curious part," Bill cut in, "is that if it weren't for fear, many of them would be happy to be on my side. Fear is a terrible thing, Daisy. Do you know that?"

"Yes," I agreed. "And they're not afraid of anything real— only of their neighbor's opinion—what the public thinks. But you'll find, Bill, that some white people in this town have been very courageous—Reverend Ogden, Gene Smith. There are others. And more will stand up," I added, hopefully.

"Well, I'll tell you this," he said, "I'm through with those useless meetings. I'm not going to attend any more."

"What can I say?" I told him. "I've quit going to those interracial groups, too. It's partly because I got fed up with their not doing anything, and also because I'm giving all my energy and time to the nine children. You know," I said, "they have to conquer a very real fear daily just to go back to that place."

"Don't think I have forgotten," Bill said. "That's why I

came out here tonight—to sort of be closer to you and feel some of that strength you exude."

We both laughed out of relief, and he was now getting ready to leave. Then I thought to ask him whether there had been any reprisals in the business. He smiled wryly and sat down again on the arm of the sofa.

"You know, Daisy," he said, "I'm the original 'Land of Opportunity' boy."

This was a reference to our State slogan, which is even engraved on our automobile license plates. Bill went on:

"I can laugh at it now, but I feel closer to tears, because just as sure as God made little green apples, there was every reason to think this State *was* on the way up. When we came here I thought of it as a sort of new frontier. It had everything that suggested progress—rich natural resources, friendly people who wanted change—look at how Grand Prairie had changed!" Grand Prairie was a vast level tract between the lower White and Arkansas Rivers where once there had been only unpainted shacks. "And look at all the new industry that was coming!" he pointed out. "I have gone all over the state making speeches, telling people about the great opportunity here if they would learn to work together to bring in new industry. But here's the rub. While I'm out making these free talks about opportunity, I'm beginning to lose my accounts!"

"No, Bill!" I said incredulously. "You, too? They're putting pressure on our *State Press* advertisers. But *you!*"

"Well," he said, "fortunately, I still have most of my business with firms outside of Little Rock, and some even outside Arkansas. But I couldn't have started a new business, especially a public relations business, at a worse time. I'd just got started when the Governor went on television and announced he was calling out the troops—as you will recall, Mrs. Bates," he added, with an affectionate grin which was more like the old Bill than anything I'd seen that night.

Bill had some very substantial accounts, but no new ones were coming in. He was preparing to leave for Europe to make a film—a project he was undertaking for an airline company that was featuring foreign travel. He hated to leave Jean and the kids just at this time. His face again clouded over, and I insisted he tell me what was wrong. "Oh," he said, "the kids have run into some static at school—but not too much as yet."

I reminded him that his children were not in Central, they were in schools in Pulaski Heights.

"But my son is William Hadley the Third," he said. "He's immediately associated with me. But it's nothing compared to what *you* cope with every day. A few crank calls, one of which, unfortunately, Missy answered." Missy was his young daughter, Margaret. "And Bill had a little brawl at school. Nothing much." He reached for his hat and was on his way out for the second time. "I'll see you when I get back from Europe, Daisy," he said. "I feel better now that I've spilled my guts to you. Just seeing you and L. C., and that battered window, with you cool as a cucumber, and L. C. routinely taking up his shotgun—all that makes me feel my troubles are lighter to carry."

As he swung out the door, I thought he had recaptured some of his old devil-may-care air, that his shoulders were thrown back a bit more cockily than when he had entered.

That night before we went to sleep, I asked L. C. what he thought it would be like to be white and see for the first time how sadistic white people can be, and how craven even the more "progressive" intellectuals and "liberal" businessmen can be.

"Maybe, hon," said L. C., "it's better to be black or brown and not be under any illusions. At least when we have a surprise it's a pleasant one. Guess it was a surprise Bill stood up like he did, for instance."

"Not really," I said. "But Jean's got a whole raft of sisters and brothers, five, I think, all over Arkansas, and she's always been very close to them. I'm not saying, but—aw, it's time to go to sleep."

Actually, the Hadleys weren't on my mind for quite a while. There was too much else. Minnijean was happy up North in school, but the other children were receiving even more openly aggressive attacks from the junior mobsters at school. The NAACP was fighting back against a raft of bills passed in the State Legislature, designed to cripple us. And L. C. and I were in a desperate fight for the survival of the *State Press*.

One day in June, 1958—I recall it was after Ernest's graduation from Central—I ran into a white friend of mine in the Federal Building post office. He was also a friend of Bill's, and moreover, as a member of one of the "First Families of Arkansas," he knew everything that went on in our town. He prided himself on being a "moderate," and was therefore a member of most of the organizations that Bill belonged to. He had been helpful to us during the crisis, although never in a public way—which is why he must remain anonymous here.

"Tell me all the scuttlebutt," I demanded.

"I'll tell you one thing," he countered, "because it's on my mind right now. I just dropped into Bill Hadley's office to ask Jean when he'd be coming back. You know, she's been keeping the office open in his absence, but today I found it closed! When I called her at home to ask how come, she spilled everything."

"Well, go on," I said.

He looked around, first over one shoulder, then the other, while he unobtrusively steered us a little farther away from persons waiting in line before a stamp window.

"What she said was, 'I just can't take it any longer'—about all the letters she had to answer from people dropping their accounts. It seems she had found whole days going by when the phone didn't ring in the office, except when someone called to make some nasty remark. So she just closed up the office and stayed home. They called there, too. 'Is this Bill Hadley's residence? Are you the wife of this nigger-lover?' That kind of thing. It's hell, because you know this is her home state, and she has always loved it. I know it hurts."

"Something has to be done," I said. "Have you tried to swing any business their way?"

He shrugged his shoulders. "Daisy, I'm afraid it will have to wait until Bill gets back. That will be soon."

Bill Hadley returned in the summer of 1958, but I didn't see him until we met by chance on board an American Airlines plane bound for Washington. That was on a morning in the spring of 1959.

"Bill!" I cried warmly, delighted to see him. "Are you going to Washington, too?"

He dropped down in the seat beside me. I chattered on about how wonderful it was to see him and what a good chance it was to have a good talk. It occurred to me that he hadn't answered my first question or made any comment at all. So I asked him again, "Where are you bound for?"

"I'm going to Washington to look for a job," he said, his jaw stiff, his eyes looking out the window as we took off. Looking down on the earth of Arkansas, he waved a mocking good-by at the ground below. "I'm not sorry to be leaving you, 'Land of Opportunity!'—opportunity gone down the drain!"

We were silent—both of us—and glad, too, I suppose, that the noise of the plane's motor and the presence of the hostess fussing over our seat belts gave us an excuse for saying nothing. I remembered, of course, that Bill had closed his public relations office. And I assumed he was going back into radio or television, or into another public relations firm.

When the plane had climbed high enough for us to look out on the edges of fluffy clouds and to settle into a steady speed, Bill told me that he was selling his home to former Governor Sid McMath. "When the sale is completed," he informed me, "we are leaving. I'm completely wiped out. Sometime I'd like to talk to you about it all—and about an experience in Europe which made me sort of come of age. But please, Daisy, not now."

I patted his arm and said nothing. We flew almost in silence to Washington, Bill alternately dozing or reading a newspaper, then throwing the paper down and moodily staring out the window.

As we walked toward the air terminal, he looked down into my eyes with a glint of his old humor and urbanity, and said, "Thanks, Daisy, for omitting the usual trite things like 'Keep your chin up,' 'If there's anything I can do for you' and so on. I've had all that—all varieties."

He turned away, then came back, adding with a grin, "Some day you'll write a book about Little Rock, I expect.

When you do, I'll give you the complete breakdown on what happened to this wide-eyed Northerner who adopted the 'Land of Opportunity' as his own—and how the customs of that land literally drove him out."

I watched him saunter over to a newsstand to buy a paper. I walked off to wait for a cab.

How many Bill Hadleys would there be before the harvest of hate sown by Faubus and Company would be gathered? How many refugees from Arkansas? I thought of the Ogden family and of how lonely the white man becomes in the South when he takes certain "unorthodox" steps. And not always, I thought, do we Negroes realize it. When we do, we don't always realize that they need our help and the feeling of our strength and support.

At that time I had many things on my mind other than writing a book. And when I began writing this personal history, I soon got the feeling it would never end. A hundred times or more I had to leave the manuscript to go to court, to face jail, to enter on a new battle or to settle an old one. The whole bitter struggle of getting the children into school in the fall of 1959 was still ahead of me, with a repetition of mobs and fears over the safety of courageous Jeff and Carlotta. But I had not forgotten Bill's promise. And knowing Bill, I knew he meant it, however lightly he had said it. I knew he would finish the story he had hardly begun.

In December of 1960, I telephoned Bill in Washington, where he was working in a Government agency. The next week, in a visit with the Hadley family, I learned for the first time the real story of his rise and fall. It is one of several stories hitherto untold, and I relate it now as a significant by-product of the "Battle of Little Rock."

This is Bill's story, told in his own words as I recorded it during my visit.

I asked him: "To start with, Bill, what was it you wanted to tell me that you experienced on your trip to Europe?"

"Oh, yes. While in Europe, I was booked, somehow, to make a couple of speeches for the State Department. Both were landmarks with me. The first was a big weekend broadcast for BBC-TV in London, on the Little Rock crisis. For about two minutes before they introduced me, they ran the old films of the mobs at Central High, and I think that was my moment of truth. That was when I realized what was going on.

"I don't think I told the British public much, as I didn't have it sorted out in my mind then. But later, in Paris, I made a speech for the Club of the Four Winds. Speakers for the club, whose members are primarily graduate students, are provided from the different embassies. I talked about forty minutes and the American embassy taped all of it. I gave them a complete, unvarnished story. Then those guys kept me there for an hour asking questions. They wanted to know how this thing could happen in a country which sets itself up as being the foremost democratic country in the world."

"I don't envy you that job," I said. "And when you got home?"

"I hit Little Rock in the midst of Faubus' campaign, in July, 1958. I didn't know how completely I was committed— even to 'go for broke.' I wasn't the same person. And Little Rock wasn't the same city I had left a couple months before. Remember that night I was out at your house? I thought things were bad then. But, when I got back from Europe, it was absolutely amazing. You could sense it from the people you saw on the streets, from their conversations. All you heard was either the election, or segregation, or both together.

"Then, the really big account I'd been trying for, which had just moved down to northwest Arkansas from up north, turned me down. And it had been in the bag. Several printing firms that had sent men to solicit business had been told, 'See our advertising agency in Little Rock.' That was us. Jean had even flown up to straighten out some details before they moved. But when I sent up the contract to be signed, it was never signed and never returned."

"Were you still called on to make speeches after you got back home?" I asked him.

"I was called on—but there was a difference. I suppose I had been in the habit of making some one hundred speeches a year, gratis. Now, everyone in Arkansas knew I was a good photographer. They'd been watching my stuff on television for five years. And the word got around that I had some films I'd made of the Brussels Fair. So I got invitations—with a stipulation. Oh, they were even apologetic about it. They wanted the pictures, all right, but they would have none of my talk. It was as if they'd said: "BLACK-OUT ON INTEGRATION. But I wasn't amused any more, so I turned them all down flat. It was about that time that I decided I should get into this fight with all four feet. And I filed to run for City Director."

"This was after Mayor Mann was replaced by a City Manager," I interrupted, "and seven City Directors were elected?"

"Right. I ran as an independent. A slate had been put up by the segregationists in one guise or another. I was running against a segregationist and someone backed by the Good

Government Committee. When I announced my decision to run, and listed all the organizations to which I belonged—including the Urban League—my phone didn't stop ringing for two days. I began to catch the full brunt of all the hatred stirred up in the course of the Governor's campaign. I don't need to tell you! You've been through it!

"After that, there wasn't much question of my ever getting additional business. I even turned photographer and sold ninety-six pictures for a dollar each to one company. Any self-respecting photographer would have shot himself first. But it was getting difficult to bring home grocery money. I tried borrowing from the bank. Then I tried friends. That's when I learned I had damn few friends left!"

"Was it then that you decided to leave Little Rock?"

"No. We still had one big account. We still had hope. And then STOP came along." STOP stood for "Stop This Outrageous Purge." It played a key role in the recall at the polls in May, 1959, of three segregationist members of the school board who had attempted to fire forty-four teachers and school administrators.

"I wasn't sure STOP was the answer," Bill went on. "The businessmen who should have taken the lead in STOP were in great measure lacking. That was what had been wrong all along. The real pillars of the community did almost no good whatever, and probably a great deal of harm, by simply keeping their mouths shut when they should have been on their toes fighting. But STOP was all we had.

"I was placing the radio and television time purchases for STOP, and fighting bitterly with some stations to get the time we wanted. But I got it. Like the half-hour show when Faubus bought the next half-hour after us. I was asked to moderate the show. I talked it over with Jean that night. We realized what would probably happen if I did moderate it, but the next day I said 'Yes.' We put on the show. It was a hot, hot night. Sweat just poured off me. At the end, strictly against instructions, I threw the script away. And I told the audience that this was the time to stand up and be counted."

"What happened?"

"Boy, oh boy! What happened? All hell broke loose the very next day. The program was on Monday night. The next afternoon's mail brought me the cancellation of a lumber company account—by now our chief bread and butter. A man I knew well—and I mean *well*—deliberately crossed the street in the middle of the block to avoid having to pass by me without speaking. And, of course, the usual deluge of phone calls. We had to take the phone off the hook."

"And how did this affect Jean?" I wondered.

"Jean was in very bad shape, almost unrecognizable from her former self. You see, it was the people of her home state who were doing this. By the way, she still has five sisters living in Arkansas—at Lonoke, Cotton Plant, Hamburg, Morrilton, and Little Rock—but only the one in Little Rock is in contact with Jean. And a sweet girl she is. Jean is all right now.

"I poured lifeblood and work into helping build that State. And it's all been thrown away."

"Did you have any idea, all through this, that there were some other white people going through this same sort of thing?" I asked. "I remember that you and Gene Smith were friends."

"I'll tell you something, Daisy," he said. "But you'll have to let me get to it in my own way. I think the worst thing that I went through was in January-February-March of last year, '59. You know, Daisy, I have a trained mind, trained for organization. Suddenly, it was as if I had no talent, no intelli-

209

gence. I thought only in spasms, in jerks. I was absolutely no good for anything. I couldn't go to the store for groceries and come back with what I was sent for—even when I had the money!"

He paused, then continued, his voice now almost inaudible.

"I couldn't sleep. I didn't sleep—for weeks at a time. I'd doze, then wander through the house at night. I was fighting a battle within myself: is this worth it, worth crucifying my family, myself? Why should I do this to myself, to my family? I'd try to think of other things—I'd pick up a book, read it, then come back to my problem—what could I do? Or I'd get in the car, turn on the radio, and just drive anywhere, anywhere at all.

"It was during this time that I almost, that I came close—very close—to committing suicide. Daisy, I'm telling you what I've never told anyone else: the gun that Gene Smith used—well, that gun was mine. I gave it to Gene when I left Little Rock. So you can imagine my shock when I heard about Gene. That's the gun I almost used on myself.

"That's about all there is to my story, Daisy. At some point you pass over the crisis. I'm not even sure why you do. But when you've passed it a lot of things are lost in your new perspective. They're not important any more.

"I was worrying myself sick about money. Why? Now I can stand in the middle of our living-room and look around at our possessions. Here's a table we love. It has much sentiment attached to it. Here are books I've had since I was a child. They don't really mean anything! Not a thing. The only thing that really means anything is people.

"And the kids? Jean and I were so busy and so worried about our own affairs, I don't think, in all sincerity, we

210

thought much about the kids for a while. Then little things began to come out. And they began to sort things out. I asked once what had happened to a friend of Missy's. They'd been inseparable. 'Oh,' she said, 'we aren't friends any more; her daddy's a segregationist.'

"Fortunately, our kids were exposed in our home to the foreign visitors you and I used to usher around Little Rock. They couldn't help but see that these terrible dark-skinned people everyone was talking about were pretty much like themselves. So this probably helped them make up their minds that their parents were right and others wrong. And by spring of '59, when Missy was thirteen and Bill fifteen, they were just as ardent civil rights advocates as we were.

"Of course, it's been rough for them, moving around as we did—we went from Winston-Salem, North Carolina, to Massachusetts, and then here to Washington. I didn't get this job with the Governmental Affairs Institute for many months. The first few months I was here the family lived with friends in Massachusetts. It was difficult for them, but I just couldn't support a family. They got here for Christmas, but we didn't exchange a single present. My son and I walked the streets of Washington for hours on Christmas Eve, looking for a tree that was small enough and cheap enough for us to buy. I had a so-called 'efficiency apartment'—hateful phrase— and had gone to the Goodwill Industries the week before to get a roll-away bed and a re-covered studio couch. The kids slept on the roll-away and Jean and I slept on the couch. It was snowing, and when we came in with the tree, without a single spangle or light for it, it was a triumph!

"The kids took to Washington right away. And now we're happy in our new Georgetown home. And, Daisy, don't let anyone tell you that integration doesn't work in Washington!

In Bill's class picture—he was graduated last year—there's every color represented. I took great pleasure in sending the picture to all the relatives in Arkansas! So now, you see, we're just an ordinary, uninteresting family in Washington."

As I stood on the snow-covered streets of Washington waiting to hail a cab and thinking of Bill's last words—"just an uninteresting family in Washington"—I noticed a group of foreign students crossing the street toward me. They paused on the sidewalk near me. One of them who had evidently been in the United States longer than the others pointed out the Capitol. They stood there looking at it longingly. I heard one of them, a lovely young woman, say, "Oh, how I've dreamed of seeing that building!"

My eyes followed theirs and rested on the Capitol dome. Now I couldn't help but feel anger for our country, which would permit racists almost to destroy a man like Bill. And I felt repulsion for the political bigots who had taken the oath of office, the likes of my own State's United States Senators John L. McClellan and J. W. Fulbright, who didn't raise their voices while Negro children were being mobbed. Yet, these same "representatives," in a left-handed way, commended the bigots by signing the so-called "1956 Manifesto" protesting the Supreme Court decision.

Looking once more toward the guests from abroad, I felt an impulse to erase the stars from their eyes. I wanted to shout, "If all the victims of lynch mobs, if all the persons murdered in and out of court by Jim Crow, if all the students beaten and jailed for simply trying to buy a cup of coffee or a Coke in America, if all of them were stacked like cordwood around the Capitol, you couldn't see that gorgeous building!"

I was moved to walk over and ask one of them, "What does that building mean to you?"

An African student dressed in his native garb looked at me startled for a moment. He replied, "It means freedom and justice."

A beautiful Indian girl, dressed in a colorful sari, then asked, "You are an American Negro—what does it mean to you?"

I couldn't answer her. I just stood there, not uttering another word. I knew all the speeches that patriotic Americans are supposed to make at such a time, but I just stood there. Sensing my confusion, they smiled and walked away, leaving me in the whirling snowstorm with the words *freedom* and *justice* sticking in my throat.

I flagged a passing taxi and went back to my hotel.

CHAPTER XV

ON WHOSE SHOULDERS

THE story of the "Battle of Little Rock" is a story of people. But it is also a story of organizations and groups that at every turn were in the forefront of the struggle, giving leadership where it was needed and whenever it became necessary.

The organization that was the prime target of all segregationists—from Governor Faubus down—was the National Association for the Advancement of Colored People. The record this organization wrote in the "Battle of Little Rock" will stand as a monument in man's eternal yearning for human rights and decency. And in this effort, Roy Wilkins will long be remembered.

As Executive Secretary of the NAACP, it fell to Mr. Wilkins to make many decisions that have since made history. Few are aware as I am of the energy and wisdom, the fortitude and patience this man brought to the leadership of the NAACP during its hour of need.

Inevitably, anxious questions were raised about the effects of the "Battle of Little Rock" on the lives of the courageous Negro youngsters who were its immediate victims. There were recurrent suggestions from the Negro and the white community that these children were being irreparably damaged by the cruelties to which they were daily being subjected, and by the publicity that inevitably surrounded them.

I discussed the matter with Mr. Wilkins. He decided to ask Dr. Kenneth B. Clark, Professor of Psychology at the College of the City of New York, and Social Science Consultant to the National Association for the Advancement of Colored People, to come to Little Rock and observe the children in varied situations.

Dr. Clark observed them together on numerous occasions and under varying conditions. He saw them at my home and in their homes, at parties and alone. He saw them with their parents and with brothers and sisters. In all, he spent sufficient time with them individually and as a group to get to know them and for them to know him.

He told me later that it was his considered judgment that, in general, these young persons showed no overt signs of personality disturbance related to the crisis. Of course there were individual differences in personality among them, as would be expected in all human beings. Some, like Minnijean Brown, were rather outgoing and expressive. Others, like Thelma Mothershed and Elizabeth Eckford, were quiet and reserved.

The outstanding thing about all of them was that their basic personality pattern determined the particular way in which they reacted to the crisis. Each one reacted to the tension and to the publicity in his own way, Dr. Clark pointed out. As a group they seemed quite resilient. And while each eventually was able to admit to Dr. Clark some feeling of anxiety or fear, no one of them at that time stated a desire to escape from the situation. In Dr. Clark's words, the stabilizing factors that prevented personality disturbances were:

"1) a sense of being a part of something meaningful and historic. (Each youngster expressed this with varying degrees of articulateness.)

"2) a generally favorable national and international publicity which they received as a group, and as individuals, bolstered their strength.

"3) a generally good and supportive relationship from their families.

"4) good *esprit de corps* among the members of the group."

In the winter of 1957 letters and messages made the rounds to certain persons in the major cities and even in smaller communities throughout the United States. The letters were virtually secret documents and were guarded as though they contained classified military information.

The contents of the letters made sense only to the recipients—all of them women. They contained the names of nine children, and next to each name were listed dress sizes, glove sizes, and other vital statistics connected with garments.

What was this all about?

The story is a simple one. Yet it contributed one of the

most important chapters in the struggle of the embattled nine. The story is as poignant for its timing as for its spiritual and material significance.

The letters and the "conspirators" involved belonged to Delta Sigma Theta, a national sorority led by Dr. Jeanne L. Noble, its President, who at the time was on the faculty of the College of the City of New York.

Under her leadership, members of the sorority chose to remember the embattled nine in a very special way at Christmas, 1957. The "coded" letters resulted in gifts of clothing and accessories for each of the nine children. They were distributed at a colorful Christmas party given by Delta Sigma Theta at the Dunbar Community Center in Little Rock. It was all a surprise. In addition to gifts of clothing there were gifts of money. The cash contributions went into a scholarship fund to assist the nine Little Rock youngsters later in their education.

Obviously the Christmas affair had a very different meaning from the Yuletide parties we were accustomed to in other years. It was a time for sadness as well as gaiety. Strange. But the time was one of suffering, as Another had suffered for mankind. If there was gaiety it lay in the certainty that His will may yet be done. . . .

And for that memorable Christmas, the women of Delta Sigma Theta Sorority will live in our hearts forever.

With the graduation of Carlotta Walls and Jefferson Thomas, on May 30, 1960, one of the most painful, turbulent, and epoch-making chapters in the history of American education came to an end.

Upon graduation the students enrolled in the following universities:

Minnijean Brown attended the Mount Sinai Hospital

School of Nursing in New York City for one year, then transferred to Southern Illinois University.

Thelma Mothershed attended Southern Illinois University in Carbondale, Illinois.

Gloria Ray attended Illinois Institute of Technology in Chicago.

Elizabeth Eckford attended Knox University in Galesburg, Illinois, for one year, then transferred to Central State College in Wilberforce, Ohio.

Carlotta Walls attended Michigan State University in East Lansing, Michigan.

Melba Pattillo attended San Francisco State University.

Jefferson Thomas attended Wayne State University in Detroit, Michigan, then transferred to City College in Los Angeles.

Ernest Green attended Michigan State University.

Terrance Roberts attended the University of California at Los Angeles.

CHAPTER XVI

HOW LONG, HOW LONG...?

In the great struggle of the colored peoples of the world for equality and independence—the struggle that is one of the truly crucial events of the twentieth century—the episode of the children in Little Rock is a landmark of historic significance.

The epic fight that was necessary for a few Negro children to gain admittance to a "white" school had a dramatic effect on America and the whole world. Only through the unbelieveable outrage at Little Rock was the world brought to a sharp realization of the shameful discrimination that the world's greatest democracy directs even against young children—in the country that boasts of being the leader of the "free world" and prides itself upon having given mankind a Constitution based upon individual dignity and liberty.

More than any other single event in many years, Little Rock demonstrated the gaping discrepancy between the Declaration of Independence—one of the precious documents of American history—and the reality of twentieth century America. Despite professions of equality, America and Americans exercise racial discrimination against millions of dark American citizens practically from the day of their birth. Even those Americans who had been fighting discrimination were startled by Little Rock. They were shocked at the utter disregard of all humanity by the segregationists, who did not shrink from using violent methods against innocent children in their struggle to maintain racial inequality.

But Little Rock came as a shock not only to many Americans, but to the world at large. Other countries knew in general about the racial inequality practiced in America, but they did not know that discrimination extended to the use of armed troops to bar teen-age children from school in defiance of court orders.

The impact on Americans and on the world was one of Little Rock's historic contributions to the over-all crusade for rights and dignity. A second contribution that Little Rock made—a contribution by no means less significant or less dramatic—was its effect upon the Negro population in the United States and particularly upon those in the South.

This was not the first really great fight waged by Negroes themselves for the validation of their civil and political rights, but it was certainly the most spectacular. It was a fight waged with legal methods, fought in the glare of public opinion and political maneuver and a fight resulting in the complete victory of a just cause.

Through the struggle and victory, Negroes tested their own strength, and won. They learned unmistakably that they possess irresistible power if they become conscious of it and unite to secure their inalienable rights. The lunch counter sit-ins, the Freedom Rides, and similar struggles in which Negroes, led by Negroes, successfully engaged after Little Rock would possibly have taken place at some time in the future in any case. But that these events occurred when they did is probably due more to the impact of Little Rock than to any other factor. Little Rock gave the signal. Events in history occur when the time has ripened for them, but they need a spark. Little Rock was that spark at that stage of the struggle of the American Negro for justice.

The 1954 Supreme Court ruling abolishing racial segregation in public education was a blow at the abuse of constitutional rights through State action obviously based upon race and color. Little Rock was the first desperate attempt by a State to maintain the old system by force of arms. It was foredoomed to failure, since the test became overnight not one of school integration, but one of the sovereignty of United States courts, and, indeed, of the survival of the American constitutional system.

L. C. and I felt from the beginning that the world was changing. We were determined to help our people and our country to contribute to that great social revolution by removing the barriers, based upon race, that had stood in our own nation for so many decades. More specifically, we were convinced that the American South, homeland to millions of darker Americans, must be the scene of major activity.

After the *State Press* was forced to close its doors, L. C. and

I were offered employment by many organizations and institutions outside of the South. One of the most attractive offers was made by Dr. Charles H. Wesley of Central State College in Wilberforce, Ohio, who offered L. C. a position as director of public relations. We turned down all the offers. Our friends asked why we chose to remain in the South. They said: "You've done your job, why don't you rest?" Our reply was that none of us, Negro or white, can afford to rest as long as Negroes suffer almost uninterrupted persecution of body and spirit.

While our friends were debating with us, the segregationists took an innocent Negro man from his home in Texas, beat him with chains, and, after carving the letters "KKK" on his chest, left him hanging by his heels as a warning to all Negroes not to press for their citizenship rights.

Tremendous changes have taken place in the field of civil rights since the Little Rock crisis. However, the United States Government, one hundred years after the Emancipation Proclamation, still finds itself grappling with the so-called "Negro problem." We are still faced with the grim fact that twenty million American Negro citizens suffer discrimination in citizenship ninety-odd years after the adoption of the Thirteenth, Fourteenth, and Fifteenth Amendments to the Constitution.

Most Americans seem to be blind to the signs of the times, which point clearly to first-class citizenship for American Negro citizens as a prime ingredient of a democratic world of liberty and equality. Even if most Americans are unseeing, the rest of the world is not. Dr. Heinrich Hellstern, head of the relief organization of the Swiss Evangelical Church, has observed fittingly:

"Little Rock is now the most famous American city besides New York and Chicago. Every boy in our country knows the name of Little Rock. Events such as you had in Little Rock and like those in New Orleans have repercussions all over the world. Your people must understand that the world has changed. They must understand that it is not just a local event—it has a world aspect. If your people will realize this, they will understand better their own federal government. I know that it is difficult and there are many tensions, but it is the task for all who are responsible for international relations."

What has happened in the five years since President Eisenhower ordered the troops into Little Rock to desegregate Central High School? Only seventy-eight Negro children have been assigned by the school board to formerly all-white junior and senior high schools!

What else has happened in these five years? The Little Rock story has been supplanted by stirring demonstrations of another kind, yet part of the same struggle for human dignity. There were the lunch counter sit-ins and the Freedom Rides that have produced memorable and heart-rending episodes.

In one such episode, a mother sat in a southern courtroom and heard a judge sentence her two sons to prison, along with their college classmates, for trying to purchase a cup of coffee at a lunch counter marked "For White Only." Tears were flowing from her eyes as she watched the police herd her sons off to jail. A white reporter leaving the courtroom paused beside her, touched her shoulder, and said, "I'm sorry." She looked at him and said: "Don't feel sorry for me. I have never been so proud of my sons as I am today."

What else has happened? There was held an election in which the two great political parties entered candidates pledged to sponsor legislative action in the field of civil rights. Since then, the President has taken affirmative executive action on a few isolated civil rights matters, but the positive leadership on broader, more meaningful measures that was promised in pre-election speeches has seemingly been forgotten. Millions of Negroes, along with many white citizens, have been left disillusioned.

What else? In 1962 a combination of southern legislators and northern Republicans threw the United States Senate into parliamentary paralysis in a maneuver to prevent civil rights legislation on the issue of voting privileges for southern Negroes who had finished the sixth grade of elementary school. Civil rights legislation has thus been postponed. Again, millions of Americans were left disillusioned. The promise of first-class citizenship to southern Negroes remains but a promise.

What else? There are stirrings among Negro Americans that the politicians ignore at the peril not only to themselves but to any government that turns its back on the lessons of history. Disillusionment breeds contempt and hostility. It fosters ugliness and undermines the democratic spirit from which our nation draws its strength.

Meanwhile, a large portion of the Negro masses is losing faith in American democracy. This is demonstrated by the growing influence on the American Negro of the nationalist organizations that have sprung up during recent years. The strongest and most widely known of these is the "Black Muslims." Whites are barred from membership. The Muslims stress the dignity of the black man. They are passive only as long as they are treated by the white man with dignity and respect. Many have joined because of a desire to belong. For the most part they have been denied a right to participate in the political and cultural development of this nation. With few exceptions, millions of Negroes live and die feeling unwanted in this country.

The leaders of these organizations claim well over two hundred thousand members. Most want no part of the white world. One Muslim told me: "We are organized for peace, but we are prepared for war." Will there one day be a bloody war on American soil—between Americans—because of the lack of forthrightness on the part of our Government to eradicate the inhuman practice of brutality and degradation now being perpetrated against American Negroes? Only America can answer this question.

And so the battle for civil rights continues. The actors on the 1957 Little Rock stage have faded from the national scene. Their places have been filled by thousands of Negro and white Americans in the crusade for equality—at the ballot box and at the lunch counter, at work and in school, in the churches and in the neighborhood, in the buses and on the beaches.

L. C. and I have committed our lives to this crusade. Together we continue to take an active part in the fight for the emancipation of the Negro in the South. That is why L. C. has accepted the position of Field Secretary of the NAACP in Arkansas. Together we look to the time when the citizens of this land will erase the shame of Little Rock, when the Constitution of the United States will embrace every man regardless of his color, when brotherhood will be more than a mere topic for an annual church sermon. For all of this, the American Negro today asks, "How long, how long . . . ?"

AFTERWORD

Daisy Bates's vivid memoir illuminates one of the key events of a historic freedom struggle. The desegregation of Little Rock's Central High School in 1957 signaled the start of an era in which increasingly widespread African American activism, often spearheaded by black youngsters, compelled federal intervention against segregationist violence. A year after President Eisenhower federalized the Arkansas National Guard and sent paratroopers from the 101st Airborne Division to Little Rock to enforce a court desegregation order, ten thousand students went to Washington, D.C., to participate in the Youth March for Integrated Schools, which called for federal enforcement of the 1954 *Brown v. Board of Education* decision; a year later twenty-five thousand students took part in a second Youth March. During the summer of 1958, NAACP Youth Council members protested against segregated lunch counters in Wichita and Oklahoma City, and in February 1960, four freshmen at North Carolina Agricultural and Technical College ignited a wave of lunch counter sit-ins that soon involved thousands of college and high-school students. In the spring of 1961, the Congress of Racial Equality launched a Freedom Ride campaign that stirred a new wave of student-led protests against segregated interstate transportation facilities and prompted President John Kennedy to send federal marshals to Montgomery, Alabama. Two years later thousands of Birmingham demonstrators, many of them teenagers, prodded the Kennedy administration to introduce legislation that became the Civil Rights Act of 1964. In the Black Belt areas of Alabama and Mississippi, organizers from the Student Nonviolent Coordinating Committee and Martin Luther King's Southern Christian Leadership Conference joined forces with grassroots voting rights proponents to orchestrate a sustained protest campaign that eventually convinced President Lyndon Johnson to push for passage of the Voting Rights Act of 1965. By the mid-1960s, the increasing militancy of youthful protesters and grassroots organizers had shifted the focus of the southern black struggle from civil rights reform to broader issues of racial identity and power.

The quiet courage of the Little Rock Nine inspired this new generation of African American activists, and they in turn were inspired by Daisy Bates, the crusading journalist and president of the Arkansas State Conference of NAACP branches. Although most histories of the modern African American freedom struggle focus on a few major confrontations between black demonstrators and white segregationists, Bates's account draws attention to the grassroots resistance to the Jim Crow system that took place in southern black communities in the years before most white Americans became aware of civil rights activism. When Bates and her husband, Lucious (better known as L. C.), began publishing the *Arkansas State Press* during the early 1940s, they consistently used the newspaper to raise the awareness of its readers, even while risking the loss of advertising from white-owned businesses. Both were NAACP members at a time when that organization was expanding its support in the South, especially in urban areas. Daisy Bates's articles on the police killing of a black soldier in 1942 reflected the growing militancy in black communities during World War II, and her gradual emergence as a leading black voice in Arkansas paralleled the emergence of other female civil rights proponents in the South, notably NAACP stalwarts Ruby Hurley, Modjeska Simkins, and Rosa Parks.

Such women set the stage for the youthful rebelliousness that made the 1950s and 1960s such an exceptional era of African American protest. Even before the Little Rock Nine became heroic figures for a new generation of African Americans, there were many indications that black high school and college students were ready to assume prominent roles in the black struggle. In April 1951, sixteen-year-old Barbara Johns led a student walkout from her high school in Farmville, Virginia, to demand an end to the inadequate facilities. Although the state NAACP office was reluctant to support the walkout, lawyers for the NAACP's Legal Defense and Education Fund did agree to add the Virginia plaintiffs to other desegregation lawsuits that were later consolidated in the *Brown* case. In the spring of 1955, fifteen-year-old Montgomery high school student Claudette Colvin became the first in her community to be arrested for refusing to give up her bus seat to a white man—a protest that was repeated later in the year by eighteen-year-old Mary Louise Smith, and, most famously, by forty-two-year-old Rosa Parks. The Reverend Martin Luther King Jr., twenty-six years old and himself not far removed from his college years, would emerge as the best-known spokesperson of the expanding black protest movement. The close relationship between Bates and the Little Rock Nine symbolized the cross-generational ties that gave the southern black movement both deep historical roots and unprecedented viability. The courage and determination displayed by the nine students were exemplary for African Americans no longer willing to acquiesce in the demeaning Jim Crow system.

The passages describing the personal feelings of the nine Little Rock students are among the most moving parts of Bates's memoir, which describes their quiet courage in the face of continued harassment and acts of intimidation. Elizabeth Eckford never abandoned her initial decision to transfer to Central High School, yet her resolve was tested on the first day of classes when she was not informed where to meet the other students. Alone on a bus bench, she confronted an angry mob, and only the timely intervention of a white woman enabled her to escape serious injury or death. Thelma Mothershed was afflicted with a heart ailment that led to a mild heart attack during that chaotic first day. Even after federal troops suppressed rioting outside the school, the students were repeatedly assaulted and verbally abused by white students. After being kicked by another student and realizing that nothing would be done to the perpetrator, Terrance Roberts considered withdrawing from school but then decided he "wasn't going to let that little pipsqueak chase me out of Central." On another occasion, Gloria Ray was attacked by boys with water pistols, which she had been told were filled with acid. Minnijean Brown was suspended and later expelled after she responded to ongoing harassment by calling a white girl who had provoked her "white trash." None of the students would withdraw voluntarily during the school year, and really all remained in the frontline of the African American struggle for justice. As Bates recounts, "In spite of the mounting attacks, the incessant humiliations, the degradations, and the harassments inflicted on the Negro students, the courageous youngsters were not to be deterred from their single-minded goal."

Bates's memoir is part of a mosaic of autobiographical accounts that remind us that the southern civil rights movement was deeply rooted in the lives of ordinary people who made extraordinary contributions to one of history's great freedom struggles. By the time the Little Rock Nine were braving violence to assert their rights, oppressed people throughout the world were freeing themselves from long-standing systems of oppression, such as the legalized racial discrimination, colonialism, and apartheid in South Africa. Although this global freedom struggle is usually depicted through the biographies of great men, such as Mahatma Gandhi, Martin Luther King Jr., and Nelson Mandela, it is best understood as an upsurge of grassroots activism by local leaders such as Daisy Bates and young people such as the Little Rock Nine. King himself recognized the crucial historical importance of the desegregation of Central High School when he told an interviewer in February 1958 that the "nine children" had given African Americans "a new sense of dignity" because of their ability to "stand up with so much courage and yet so much dignity in the midst of all of the abuses that they've had to confront." A few months later King visited Bates in Little Rock and then invited her to be Women's Day speaker at Dexter Avenue Baptist Church in Montgomery. "We have had many men and they have been warmly received," King informed Bates. "But at this time, if we could have a woman who everyone KNOWS has been, and still is in the thick of the battle from the very beginning, never faltering, never tiring . . . it would be the greatest impetus, the greatest inspiration, the greatest challenge to the women to carry on." Dexter's secretary, Lillie Hunter, later recounted that Dexter was "jammed to an overflowing capacity" for Bates's talk. "She was genuinely enjoyed," Hunter reported, based on "the responsive 'Amens' and the frequent foot patting."

Bates's memoir demonstrates that courageous, individual acts of resistance against injustice can lead to important, if not conclusive, victories. As inferior, racially segregated educational

231

institutions continue to limit the opportunities of millions of students, her story will serve as a source of inspiration for future participants in the long struggle for human freedom.

CLAYBORNE CARSON
Professor of history and director,
Martin Luther King Jr., Research and Education Institute
Stanford University

INDEX

235

DAISY BATES (1913?-1999) and her husband published the *Arkansas State Press* from 1941 to 1959. Bates revived the paper in 1984 and sold it in 1988. She served on the NAACP's national board from 1957 to 1970. In 1957, the Associated Press chose her as its Woman of the Year in Education and one of the top ten newsmakers in the world. Her prominence as one of the few female civil rights leaders of the period was recognized by her selection as the only female to speak at the Lincoln Memorial at the March on Washington on August 28, 1963. In 2001, the Arkansas legislature enacted a provision that recognizes the third Monday in February as "Daisy Gatson Bates Day."

CLAYBORNE CARSON is a professor of history and founding director of the Martin Luther King Jr. Research and Education Institute at Stanford University. In 1985, the late Coretta Scott King invited Carson to direct a long-term project to edit and publish King's papers. The King Papers Project has produced five volumes of a projected fourteen-volume comprehensive edition of King's speeches, sermons, correspondence, publications, and unpublished writings. Carson is the author of a number of books, including *In Struggle: SNCC and the Black Awakening of the 1960s*, winner of the Frederick Jackson Turner Award.